GARDENERS' WORLD
FRUIT GARDEN

In the same series
Gardeners' World Vegetable Book
The Gardeners' World Cottage Garden

GEOFF HAMILTON
GARDENERS' WORLD
G·FRUIT GARDEN·D

DRAWINGS BY
LORNA TURPIN

BRITISH BROADCASTING CORPORATION

Published by the
British Broadcasting Corporation
35 Marylebone High Street
London W 1 M 4AA

ISBN 0 563 20146 0
First published 1983
© Geoff Hamilton 1983

Set in ten on eleven Garamond
by Phoenix Photosetting, Chatham
and printed in Great Britain
by Mackays of Chatham Ltd

CONTENTS

1 INTRODUCTION

When Eve persuaded Adam to take a bite from the notorious forbidden apple, she wasn't doing him any favours. Apart from getting them thrown off the best allotment site the world has ever known, that was no Cox's Orange Pippin she was offering. It must have tasted pretty grim!

In those far off days, East Malling Research Station was still a fair way off and Mr Bramley was but a seedling. The ancestors of our modern varieties were small, hard, juiceless globes of acid.

The Romans first brought apple cultivation to this country and we've come a very long way since then. For centuries men have researched, selected and improved on the wild varieties of fruit and today, modern varieties and methods of cultivation bear little resemblance to the fruits our ancestors ate.

As with all branches of science, the greatest strides have been made in the last hundred years, and research still continues.

Year by year, fruit has become bigger, juicier and better flavoured than ever before.

Yet, of all branches of gardening, nothing is shrouded in more mystery and mumbo-jumbo than fruit growing. There is no doubt in my mind that many gardeners are put off growing their own, by the sheer complication of the available advice.

With this in mind I set about trying to simplify the whole business and to work out a blueprint for the home gardener and particularly for the very small plot.

We've looked into most of the fruits popular with home-gardeners and many of the experiments you will have seen on *Gardeners' World* programmes. Alas, time is never on our side in the half-hour we're allotted each week, so this book is intended to expand that information.

Many of the new techniques I suggest were originally developed for the commercial grower and adapted to suit the garden, and I must take this opportunity to thank the many commercial growers, nurserymen and scientists who have freely given me help and advice and who have taken such a keen interest in the work we do at Barnsdale. Many of the techniques described here are adapted from the work done at East Malling Research Station to whom I extend my grateful thanks.

I make no claims that this is an entirely comprehensive manual of fruit-growing. Indeed, that is precisely what I have set out to avoid. What I hope and believe you will find in the following pages is a simple, easy-to-follow method of growing successfully most of the fruits suitable for modern, small gardens. Pruning, training and feeding systems have been simplified and I've tried to avoid the necessity for a garden shed full of pills and potions.

One thing our work at Barnsdale has proved beyond doubt is that growing delicious, fresh fruit, the like of which you will never buy in the shops, is a whole lot easier than you think.

2 PLANNING

It would be unrealistic to suggest that a new fruit garden will not set you back a few bob. By the time you've laid out for the trees and bushes, the stakes and ties, the manure and fertiliser and the necessary tools, your cheque book will begin to feel the strain. On the other hand, over a long period they'll repay you well. Tree fruit has a cropping life of upwards of thirty years, while most bush fruit should still be producing good crops after ten or twelve. Two good reasons why it's worth spending a bit of time in planning and preparation.

Soil and site

While gardeners have no choice concerning either their soil or the location in which they grow fruit, both could well have an important influence on what is grown.

Fruit trees and bushes flower early on in the season, when there may be a good chance that frost will destroy the blossom. Naturally, if this happens, there will be no fruit either. But it is possible to avoid frost damage to some degree.

Barnsdale is situated just about in the middle of the country, so we have a fair chance of suffering from late frosts and gardeners in the north even more so. In an attempt to avoid the worst effects of cold weather, I've tried several different varieties of fruit of all kinds to try to find out which are most frost resistant. Naturally, those varieties that flower late are less subject to damage and these are listed in the recommended varieties for each type of fruit. The further north you live, the more important it is to choose these varieties.

Cold winds will also affect the amount of fruit you harvest at the end of the season. Again, wind can physically damage blossom, and it will also discourage pollinating insects from their invaluable work. On an exposed site, it will pay to filter the wind with a windbreak.

In very small gardens a fence or wall will provide quite adequate shelter. But, in a larger garden, a more permeable barrier is preferable.

When a strong wind meets a solid barrier, it tends to whoosh up one side, do a couple of quick double-somersaults, whistling straight down to ground level again to continue on its merry way (1). During the initial acrobatics, it can actually increase in speed.

A semi-permeable windbreak on the other hand, will simply slow the wind down to an acceptable level, without stopping it dead (2). So, a close hedge or a length of propriet-

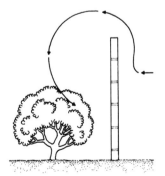

1 *Wind tends to 'jump' a solid barrier and eddy on the other side*

9

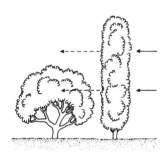

2 *A permeable hedge will filter the wind and slow it down*

ary plastic windbreak provides more effective protection than a wall. Plastic windbreak netting is not the most attractive material in the world, I have to admit, but it's a very good temporary measure while a hedge is growing up.

Almost any hedging plant will do, since even those that lose their leaves in winter still make an effective enough barrier. However, if your garden is small, I would advise against privet. It's a voracious eater and will swallow up all the water and nutrients from the soil within about ten feet, giving no chance to other more attractive or productive plants. It also seems to harbour many more pests and diseases than other plants.

Of course, solid barriers do have one distinct advantage. They provide a perfect framework for training all types of fruit. In a small garden, I'd use every available wall for growing fruit – indeed I do. A south- or west-facing wall or fence is ideal for the more tender fruits like peaches and nectarines, while a north or east wall can be used for Morello cherries or the briar fruits like blackberries or loganberries. They look good, they'll produce a lot of fruit and, perhaps more important these days, they take up virtually no room at all.

The one other important consideration when choosing which fruits you are to grow and where you'll grow them is the amount of light they will receive. It must be said that all fruit plants *prefer* a sunny position, but some will tolerate a shady spot and still produce quite acceptable crops.

If there's a shady spot in your garden, as there is in most, you'll still be able to fill it with briar fruits, to a lesser extent with raspberries and certainly with rhubarb. Currants will yield a good crop in a shady spot, and so will gooseberries, but they'll be a week or two later than those planted in the sun.

Apples, pears, plums and sweet cherries all need a sunny position in order to ripen the fruit buds and it's essential for strawberries too. In trials at Barnsdale, there was a thirty per cent reduction in crop when I planted normal varieties in the shade, though alpine varieties like *Alexandria* and *Baron Solemacher* thrived and yielded well.

It's plain that by careful selection of the right position and choice of varieties, there is no place in the garden that need be unproductive.

Soil preparation
Good soil preparation is vital. It really is daft to spend a lot of money on trees and bushes and then immediately to reduce the chances of a good cropping life by skimping on the work of planting them.

Most fruit will grow well on all but the extremes of soil and, even if your garden is blessed with very heavy clay or light, poor sand, it can still be improved to give acceptable yields.

The first and most important essential is a good, deep root-run and free drainage. Bear in mind that in this country, plants have to suffer extremes of climate. In the summer it is possible, though the sun-lovers may not agree, to experience prolonged periods of drought, which are often followed in winter by drenching, mud-making rain and snow. Temperatures can vary between the nineties in the summer to minus twenty degrees in the winter.

With a good, deep root system, trees and bushes can take all this and still come back for more. But if the roots are near the surface, they will suffer badly.

Obviously, once the trees and bushes are planted, there is no chance to cultivate deeply, so it pays hands down to ensure that conditions are right beforehand. It's not easy work to be sure, but it only has to be done once. You may even get to enjoy it.

It is often recommended that holes should be dug about two feet square, breaking up the bottom and adding a bit of manure or peat. On heavy soils, particularly, this could be worse than useless.

Those isolated holes could act just like a sump. There is a tendency for all the drainage water from the surrounding land to find its way into the hole and fill it with root-rotting water. No plant will do well under those conditions. There is no substitute for preparing the whole site by deep, double digging.

On some deep, lightish soils, it may be possible to get away with single digging, but these conditions are very much the exception rather than the rule. If your soil is like that, offer up a prayer to Mother Nature and send a fiver to the Gardeners' Benevolent Society in gratitude. You'll be very much in the minority.

Generally, and especially in new gardens, the top few inches may look okay, but underneath there'll be a solid 'pan' of hard, compacted soil.

Very often, on new estates, the builders, in their wisdom, will spend a year running over the soil with gargantuan machines and, just before they hand over the house to the unsuspecting innocent who hopes to make a garden of it, they'll spread a few inches of topsoil over it. That's like sweeping the dirt under the carpet.

At Barnsdale, I had the same problem but for a different reason. Here, the land had been ploughed to the same depth for donkey's years. In this case, the ploughshare tends to glaze

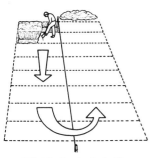

3 *Divide the plot in half, work down one side, turn round and work back down the other*

the soil at the ploughing depth, creating just the same sort of hard pan. It *must* be broken, and the only way is to double dig.

The best way to do this is to divide the area in half with a tight garden line (3). Take out a trench at one end across half the plot, making it about 2ft (60cm.) wide and one spade deep. I keep a 2ft (60cm.) cane handy (4) to mark out each successive trench enabling me to dig the site level first time over (5).

The soil from the first trench is barrowed over to the other half of the plot, preferably just off the area to be dug. It can then be used to fill in the final trench (6).

Dig over the bottom of the trench with a fork (7), breaking

4 *Keep a 2ft cane handy to mark out the trenches*

5 *Dig the first trench one spade deep and shovel out the 'crumbs'. All this soil is barrowed away*

6 *The soil from the first trench is dumped near to the other side of the plot, at the same end*

7 *Break up the bottom of the trench to the full depth of the fork*

up the soil to its full depth and then put a generous layer of organic matter on the top (8). Ideally, you should also spread the organic matter over the surface of the next bit of soil you're going to dig, so that you also work some into the top layer too.

Then mark out the next trench 2ft (60cm.) wide and dig this out in the same way. The soil from this trench is thrown forward to fill the first one (9). Try to dig it as level as you can to save yourself some work later. Obviously the dug soil will be quite a bit higher than that surrounding it, but it will settle later.

Continue down the first half of the plot in this way and, when you get to the end, simply turn round and work back again. At the end of it, you'll feel very pleased with yourself, a whole lot fitter and probably ready for a well-deserved pint.

The reason for digging in organic material is nothing to do with its fertiliser content. It acts purely as a soil conditioner, opening up the soil, and retaining water and plant food, while allowing the excess to drain away. So, any sort of bulky organic matter will do. Farmyard manure is best, provided it's well rotted. Fresh stable manure, for example, is very powerful stuff and may scorch the tender young roots.

But farmyard manure is not too readily available these days, so you may have to resort to something else.

Good, home-made garden compost is ideal and certainly the cheapest alternative. If you haven't got a supply, use spent mushroom compost, which is often available at garden centres or straight from the mushroom farm. Wool shoddy is fine and should be easy to come by in the north or, as a rather expensive alternative, use peat, composted bark or one of the proprietary

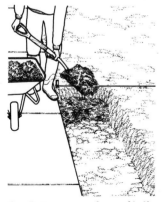

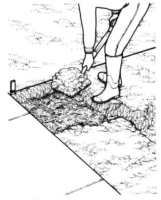

8 *Put a generous layer of bulky organic matter in the bottom of the trench*

9 *The soil from the next trench is thrown forward to fill the first one*

organic soil conditioners. Straw is not to be recommended unless it has been composted for some time. The bacteria that rot down any material nitrogen – a basic plant food responsible for shoot growth – as their fuel. If the material is uncomposted and contains no nitrogen, they will extract it from the soil to the detriment of the plants.

Generally, there will be no need to lime the land before planting. Most fruit prefers a slightly acid soil, so lime is only necessary if you know the soil to be very acid (below pH6).

After digging, it's best to leave the soil to settle for a while. The length of time will depend largely on the weather, but four or five weeks should be sufficient. However, bear in mind that planting of bare-rooted trees must be done between November and the end of March, so don't allow yourself to be delayed.

Decorative fruit

My previous recommendations for soil preparation and the choice of position in your garden have assumed that you look upon your fruit garden as something purely productive. In small gardens, this may not always be the case. Often, there is no room for the luxury of a purely productive area and fruit and vegetables have to be grown in the lawn or the borders where they must enhance the ornamental effect too. Fruit trees are ideally suited as 'dual-purpose' plants. The blossom of apples, pears, plums and cherries is a delight in the spring and there is the added bonus of colour from the autumn foliage and the fruit itself.

It may be then, that your fruit must be sited where it will give the most decorative effect. In many cases, this may mean that you should not expect quite such a good crop. Other plants, particularly grass, will compete with the trees and will certainly reduce the crop to some extent.

We all remember the 'old-fashioned' orchard, where big, knarled old trees grew in deep, lush grass, often grazed by sheep, chickens or geese. Very pleasant places they were too, and there must be something to be said for it as a garden feature if you have the room. But, modern research has shown that this is very far from the best way to grow productive trees. The grass competes for water and nutrients, robbing the trees at every turn. The modern method is to spray out that attractive grass so that the trees can reap the full benefit of fertiliser and water. I don't intend to enter into a philosophical argument about the relative morality of each method, but the 'scorched earth' policy is certainly the most productive in terms of fruit.

So, in small gardens we must make a compromise. If your tree is growing in grass, cut a bed round it for at least a couple of feet and preferably more, to reduce the competition in the early stages (10). Feed a little earlier than you normally would, say in early February. This way, the fertiliser can get down to the roots before the grass starts growing.

If the lawn is already established before the tree is planted, there is no alternative but to plant in the way I suggested was 'worse than useless'. Simply dig a hole, break up the bottom and add manure. However, planting in grass makes the problem not quite so acute, since the grass roots will suck up quite a lot of water. On all but the heaviest soils, you'll get away with it.

Trained fruit can also be a very decorative feature in the garden. I have already suggested that fan-trained or espalier trees can be used to cover otherwise bare walls. All they need is the support of a few wires fixed to battens on the wall or fence. Think also of using cordon-trained apples and pears as a division between perhaps the vegetable and ornamental gardens. You'll never grow a more decorative or productive hedge.

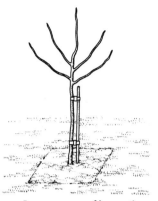

10 *Leave an area of bare soil around young trees growing in grass*

Fruit cages

While in the planning stage, it's worthwhile thinking about growing all your fruit together in a fruit cage. There's no doubt that the worst pests of fruit are our feathered 'friends'. They will strip the fruit buds from soft-fruit bushes in particular, and they'll often spoil the fruit too. Alas, they tend to get up in the morning a lot earlier than even the keenest gardener, and they have as much of a liking for a fresh strawberry or a juicy pear as we do. The problem is what to do with them. While most of us would think nothing of spraying a million greenfly out of existence, we could never bring ourselves to poison a bird. The only answer is to scare them off or physically protect the fruit from them.

With this in mind, I carried out a whole series of bird-scaring experiments at Barnsdale. I have used every sort of strange device imaginable, from a rotating gentleman of patently Italian origin who would frighten a Liverpool docker on a dark night, to highly-coloured inflatable snakes. Frankly, none of them worked for more than a day or two. Even moving them round had little effect, but inside my fruit cage, apart from the odd accident when a bird somehow managed to find his way in, I had no trouble.

A fruit cage needs careful planning, and the tendency is always to try to cram in more than it will really take. But, with a little careful manipulation, it's amazing what they will

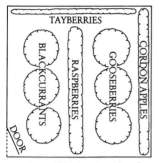

11 *A possible planting plan for a fruit cage 25ft × 25ft*

grow. Mine is 25ft×25ft (7.5×7.5m.) and I find room for eight cordon apples and pears, three blackcurrants, three gooseberries, a tayberry and a row of raspberries. Strawberries are very easy to cover with loose netting, so I grow those outside the cage (11).

Of course, I appreciate that a fruit cage once again puts up the expense. But with plastic netting, they will last a lifetime and they are, in my experience, the only completely successful method of controlling birds.

Buying plants

Perhaps the most important stage in establishing your new fruit garden, is the selection and buying of plants. It's a job that warrants a lot of head-scratching and, when you've made up your mind, a bit of travelling too.

Though you may have to shell out a fairly substantial sum, there's one great consolation.

While every manufactured product you buy will start to diminish in value and usefulness just as soon as you leave the shop, living plants actually do the reverse. Year by year they will continue to improve and increase in value and cropping potential. They are a cast iron, gilt-edged investment that will give you years of pleasure and tons of fresh fruit.

But, they need an investment in terms of cash and an even greater one in terms of labour. So, to ensure that you get the full value of both, it is *essential* to start off with the very best. In fact, the best will rarely cost more and often less.

The first golden rule in my view, is to buy your plants from a fruit specialist. If possible, go and see the trees or bushes before you buy them. If that's impossible, make sure that the covering letter with your order gives a detailed specification of what you want. On the whole, the nursery business is a highly ethical one, but if the grower is made aware that you know very well the difference between a good plant and a bad one, he'll be bound to look after you.

Start by getting hold of the catalogue, and carefully selecting the varieties you need. Bear in mind that you can greatly spread the harvesting period of most fruits by growing different varieties.

If you're ordering apples or pears, a pollinator is essential. None will set a full crop of fruit on their own pollen, so you'll need at least two different varieties that flower at the same time and are capable of pollinating each other – more about that in chapter 5. Some plums and cherries will also need a pollinator, though not all, so here it is possible to get away with just one tree. All soft fruit is self-fertile.

When ordering apples, it's also worth bearing in mind that the early-cropping varieties won't keep well. So, if you want apples after Christmas, you'll need a late cropper too. You'll also need to state the rootstock you require and that's all explained in chapter 5 too.

Most fruit is subject to attack from virus diseases, and these are real killers. Diseased trees and bushes will produce poor crops and will eventually fail altogether. The diseases are carried in the main by aphids or other small bugs, so an effective spraying programme will generally prevent them. But it's important to ensure that you buy clean stock to start with.

Many types of fruit are controlled by the Ministry of Agriculture Certification Scheme, which ensures that fruit trees and bushes for sale are free from disease when they leave the nursery. You should never buy fruit trees or bushes unless they have been certified under the scheme.

It is a common misconception that fruit trees take seven years to come into bearing and that if you therefore buy a three-year-old tree, you reduce the waiting time by that amount. In fact, the complete reverse is true. On modern, semi-dwarfing rootstocks, trees will generally start cropping in their second year. You may even get some fruit in the first. It is also true to say that the older a tree is, the longer it takes to establish and the longer it takes to bear fruit. So, start with 'maidens' – one-year-old trees – or at the most, two-year-olds.

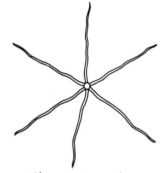

12 *Choose new trees with branches evenly spaced all round*

The one advantage with two-year-olds is that they will already have been pruned to shape, while maidens may not. Indeed, a one-year-old tree may be nothing more than a single stem with no side-branches at all. Don't worry about that. They'll produce branches in the year after planting and you'll have the opportunity of shaping the framework exactly as you want it, which is not a difficult task at all. If your chosen tree does have side-branches, make sure you choose one that is well shaped. You're looking for a sturdy main stem with the branches coming out almost at right-angles and evenly spaced round the stem like the spokes of a wheel (12) and (13).

If you are buying fan-trained or espalier trees and you don't fancy the idea of shaping them from scratch, you will have to buy them a bit older.

The same rules apply to bushes. Gooseberries and redcurrants are grown on a stem and look like the ideal apple tree in miniature. A good clean stem and well-spaced branches.

Blackcurrants and the briar fruits grow from the base of the plant, so all you need to look for here is a good, healthy collection of stems, and, of course, that Ministry certificate of cleanliness.

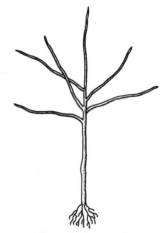

13 *The angles between the branches and the trunk should be wide*

3 PLANTING

With all the really hard preparation work behind you, planting the trees and bushes is sheer joy. Even if the plants have no leaves on them at planting time, they seem to make an immediate impact on the garden. It begins to look 'lived-in'.

I have detailed the various spacings and any special points to watch for under the separate headings in the following chapters, but since the general techniques are the same for nearly all trees and bushes, I include them here.

Time to plant

Time was, when all woody plants had to be planted during the dormant season between November and the end of March. All that has changed with the introduction of container plants which entirely dispense with a planting season. They can go in at any time of the year.

However, my own experience is that bare-rooted plants tend to get away faster. Since there is also a more limited list of varieties grown in containers generally, you'll get more choice if you can curb your enthusiasm and wait until the dormant season.

There is also the point that specialist fruit-tree raisers mainly still offer their trees bare-rooted because they are then eligible for the Ministry Certification Scheme, so I think that bare-rooted plants are to be strongly recommended.

The best time to plant them is in early November, and certainly before Christmas. At that time of the year, there is still a little warmth in the soil and they will probably make a little root growth before the onset of the real winter. So, send away for the catalogue in plenty of time, and get your order in early, specifying a November delivery if at all possible. Even better, visit the nursery, select the plants you want and watch them being lifted.

By the well-known 'Law of the Cussedness of Nature', my plants always arrive either when it's pouring with rain, when there's two feet of snow on the ground or when I simply *have* to spend the weekend visiting my Mum for the sake of sheer survival. You should never plant when the soil is frosted or very wet so, if you do get caught out like this, straightaway make a temporary home for them. Ideally, they should be 'heeled-in' in some out-of-the-way corner of the garden, but you should only do this if the soil conditions are suitable. If there is frost in the ground or it's covered in snow or very wet, it's better to leave the plants in their packing until things improve. Just

14 *To heel plants in temporarily, start by digging a trench and sloping the soil up at the back*

15 *Take the plants out of their bundles and lay them at an angle in the trench*

16 *Cover the roots with soil and firm it down gently*

put them as they are in a frost-free shed or garage. They'll be fine like that for a few days at least.

Heeling-in is really just a case of covering the roots with soil. Simply dig a trench and lay the plants out so that the roots are in the trench and their stems leaning at an angle on the mound of soil you have dug out (14) and (15). Then cover the roots with the soil from the next trench and gently tread them down (16). The idea of heeling them in at an angle is simply to prevent them blowing about in the wind.

If, when you unpack the plants the roots seem dry, always soak them in a bucket of water for an hour or two before heeling in or planting.

If soil conditions are too wet for heeling in or planting for some time, you'll have to use another method. Unwrap the plants, lay them out flat on the ground or lean them against the fence and cover the roots with a good, thick layer of moist peat or soil, if you can find any that is in suitable condition. Then cover the heap of peat with an old tarpaulin or something similar to protect the roots from frost. Heeled in by either of these methods, the plants can wait several weeks until you're ready for planting.

Container-grown plants will be perfectly happy just standing in their pots. They'll need to be supported to prevent them falling over, and they will probably need watering if the weather is dry.

Before planting trees, you'll need a good stout stake and a tree-tie. The stake should always be thicker than the trunk of the tree and long enough to reach the part of the stem where the first branches start when it's driven about 18in. (45cm.) into the ground.

In fact, some commercial fruit growers now plant small trees without a stake at all, but I believe that this is simply an economy and not really to be recommended. If the tree moves around in the wind, it works a hole in the soil around the main stem. Water fills the hole and remains right on the crown of the root system. In the winter especially, this can cause rotting and a fungus disease rather dramatically known as 'The Death'. Sounds like something out of *Treasure Island*!

If you're planting bare-rooted trees, dig out a hole big

17 *Dig a hole large enough to take the full spread of the roots*

18 *Drive the stake in before planting to avoid root damage*

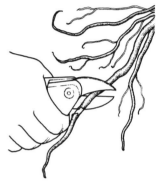

19 *Trim back any broken or damaged roots*

enough to take the full spread of the roots (17) and deep enough so that the tree sits comfortably just an inch or so lower than it grew on the nursery. You'll easily be able to see a soil mark which will tell you exactly how deep it should be.

Before setting the tree in the hole, drive the stake in to the required height (18). If you do it afterwards, you'll be quite likely to damage the roots. If the roots are broken or split, prune them back with a sharp pair of secateurs leaving a clean cut which will heal all the quicker (19).

Now sprinkle a good handful of bonemeal on the heap of soil you have dug out (20). This is a phosphate fertiliser that will release its nutrients over a long period. Phosphate is the element that plants use to promote root growth, so it's just what the doctor ordered at this stage.

Cover the roots initially with the very best of the topsoil you have dug out (22). It should be reasonably dry and crumbly so that it works down between the fine roots. Now grab hold of the stem and vibrate it up and down to make sure that plenty of the fine soil works its way down between the roots (23).

If your soil is heavy, this may be a bit of a tall order, though you should never, of course, plant when it is very wet. If you can't find good, crumbly soil, work a little moist peat in around the roots and mix a bit more with the soil you dug out.

Then half-refill the hole and firm gently with your boot (24). Plants need to be planted firmly, but you must ensure that you don't overdo the firming, especially on heavy land, or

20 *Sprinkle a good handful of bonemeal on the soil you have dug out*

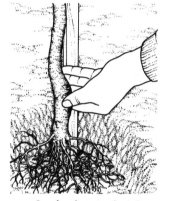

21 *Set the plant in the hole ensuring that the joint between rootstock and variety is well above soil level*

22 *Cover the roots with the best of the topsoil you have dug out*

23 *Shake the tree gently up and down so that soil trickles between the roots*

24 *Tread the soil around the roots, finish refilling and tread again*

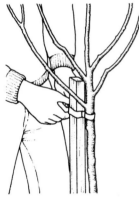

25 *Fix the tree to the stake using a special plastic tree-tie*

it will set like concrete when it dries out. The hole can now be refilled completely, firming again afterwards.

Having just paid for the tree, it's a temptation to skimp on the tie and to use a piece of nylon string or even wire. Never do it. It's more than worthwhile investing another couple of bob in a proper plastic tree-tie (25). Wire or string will cut into the bark and wear it away eventually. If it cuts through all round, the tree will die.

A proper plastic tie is wide and flexible, so there is no danger of this, though in future years, it's worth checking them and letting them out a little as the diameter of the stem expands. After fixing, the tie should be tacked to the stake, (*never* to the tree), just to stop it slipping down. A cheaper alternative is to use a cut-up polythene compost bag folded into a strip but it does rather offend the eye.

With the planting completed, level the soil neatly round the tree, just prick over the surface with a fork to get rid of your footmarks, and mulch around the stem with a layer of well-rotted manure or compost.

Planting trees from containers differs slightly. Firstly, as I have already mentioned, they can be planted at any time of the year, since the roots won't be disturbed.

If you're planting in the summer, give the root ball a good drink and let it drain for a few minutes. I feel a bit churlish by insulting your intelligence to remind you to remove the container, but it is less uncommon than you think for trees to be planted complete with plastic bag. So, forgive me if I include the advice – purely for the other feller, of course.

Most fruit trees are sold in plastic bags, which can be cut off quite easily. I like to put the knife inside the bag and cut outwards to avoid butchering the roots. It's often advised to put the plant in the hole before cutting the bag off, but I find this awkward and quite unnecessary. If the tree has a good root system, the root-ball will hold together anyway. If it doesn't, take it back from whence it came.

Don't disturb the root-ball at all when you plant, but simply put it in the hole at the correct level, refill halfway, firm and top up. Then lightly firm again as before and mulch. The one thing to watch out for with container-grown trees is that you don't firm on top of the ball since this could also lead to root damage. Just tread the soil in around it.

If you're planting in the summer, you should water well after planting and keep an eye on the soil to ensure that it doesn't dry out subsequently.

Planting gooseberry and redcurrant bushes is exactly the same except that there is no need for a stake. The remainder of the soft-fruit clan need specialised treatment which is explained fully in the relevant chapters.

After planting, there is just one common pest to guard against – Brer Rabbit. These delightful, furry little animals are a real pain, especially in country gardens. In the winter, when there's not a lot of greenstuff about, they will nip into your new fruit garden and make a fine meal of the bark. As with the warning about tree-ties, if they chew all the way round, and believe me they generally do, the tree will die.

There are special plastic tree-guards available that will efficiently frustrate their efforts or, if you have a bit of old wire netting knocking about, you can make a cylinder of it around the stem and just staple it to the stake.

At Barnsdale, we have one even worse problem from deer. They comfortably leap the four-foot wire-netting fence and simply strip off every bit of bark there is. Alas, there is no answer short of replacing the fence with a ten-foot one or a barbed-wire entanglement.

4 CULTIVATION

The detailed cultivation techniques for different types of fruit vary quite a bit, so I have included most of this information under their separate headings. There are, however, several points in common regardless of the fruit you are growing.

Feeding

With the possible exception of strawberries on very fertile soil, all fruit trees and bushes need feeding. Generally, this is a once-a-year job so it's not that onerous.

I must say that I've been a bit put off by the general recommendations for feeding. They are often over-complicated and quite honestly, I find it difficult to understand how it is possible to be so dogmatic. Unless you are prepared to go to the lengths of taking a soil test every year, it's impossible to know exactly how much of any particular element is needed and I don't believe that most gardeners have the time to do this.

In my view, it's much more realistic to use a compound fertiliser like Growmore or blood, fish and bone, than to fiddle about with 'straights' like sulphate of ammonia or superphosphates.

I suppose it must be admitted that this may not produce the maximum yields, but I'm sure that most gardeners would be quite happy with ninety-five per cent. It may also be argued that a more hit-or-miss method is more expensive because some fertiliser may be wasted. But, if you take into account the annual soil tests and the fact that it would be necessary to keep in stock at least three different fertilisers, I think it works out cheaper in the end. So, in every case, I use a compound fertiliser. It seems to work well enough for me.

Accurate application of fertilisers is a bit more tricky. The recommendations I have given are in ounces per square yard and I appreciate that few gardeners are going to venture into the fruit plot with the kitchen scales to weigh every ounce. There's a much easier method.

Weigh out an ounce of general fertiliser and put it into a plastic coffee-cup, making a mark with an indelible pen on the side of the cup where it comes to. Repeat with two, three and four ounces and you have a ready-made measure (26). It's easy enough to roughly mark out a square yard with a couple of 3ft (90cm.) canes.

When applying fertiliser to established trees, there's little point in putting it too close to the trunk. All the tiny feeding roots are situated at the ends of the main roots and these will

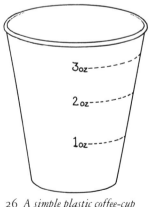

26 *A simple plastic coffee-cup fertiliser measure*

be some distance from the tree. Look at the extent of the branches and apply the fertiliser in a broad circle around the tree roughly at that distance away from the trunk (27).

Timing of fertiliser application is a great bone of contention amongst professional fruit growers. For years, argument has raged about the best time to apply different 'straight' fertilisers. If you're using a general mixture, the best time to use it is the end of February. At that time the soil is moist, so the food will quickly be taken down to the root zone ready for the start of growth in early spring.

Mulching

Apart from the nitrogen, phosphates and potash needed in quantity by plants, they also need some elements in minute quantities. These are known as 'trace' elements. Though they need very little, they are nonetheless vital to healthy growth and deficiencies can cause problems. However, if trees and bushes are mulched every year with manure or compost, it is very unlikely that deficiencies will occur. Both these materials would normally contain plenty of the necessary chemicals.

27 Apply fertiliser in a wide band, roughly at the furthest extent of the branches

Mulching has other great benefits. Firstly, the material will eventually be taken down to the lower levels of the soil by earthworms and other soil organisms and by the action of rain. Here it will rot down to form humus to maintain the soil in the good, fertile condition it was when you planted. Deep down below the surface it will be retaining water and plant food, improving drainage and aeration and providing a home for countless millions of beneficial soil organisms.

The layer on the surface has an important function too. While its porous nature will allow rain water to penetrate to the roots, it will prevent evaporation and also slightly raise the temperature of the soil.

As if all that were not enough, it will also save you hours of weeding by suppressing weeds before they get a chance to establish themselves. The value of mulching can't be over-estimated (28).

28 Mulching with manure or compost adds trace elements and helps conserve water

Watering

All fruit consists of a high percentage of water, so a moist soil at the right time of the year can greatly increase the size and yield of fruit trees and bushes.

Obviously, all plants need water for growth too and should never be allowed to dry right out. In very dry years, this could mean hand-watering. Imagine the enormous leaf area of a big old apple tree, and you'll see that it may take quite a lot of water to replace what it loses in hot weather.

It's almost pointless standing in the garden with a hose when it needs large amounts of water, and a watering-can is out of the question. Indeed, just wetting the top layers of soil could do more harm than good. In this case, the young roots come up to the surface in search of water and are then more prone to drying out in hot weather. The golden rule is, if you are going to water at all, make a job of it and put on plenty.

The only sensible way to do this is with some form of irrigation system. I use a pulsating-head sprinkler on top of a long tube mounted on a tripod (29). You can get them at most garden centres and they are quite reasonably priced. The advantage of the tall sprinkler is that it will water over the top of soft-fruit crops like blackcurrants, so you can cover a much bigger area at a time. It can, of course, still be used for watering the lawn, so there's no need to buy another sprinkler.

Remember that some councils insist that you buy a licence for this equipment and that in periods of acute drought, watering in the garden may be banned. In this case I'm afraid there is nothing to do but grin and bear it.

The amount of water to apply and the best time to do it are more difficult decisions for the home gardener than for the professional who would have sophisticated measuring equipment and complicated tables to help him. The ordinary gardener must rely to some degree on his 'nose'.

In periods of prolonged drought like we had in 1976, serious water shortage occurs and this is enough to affect the growth of trees and bushes and the development of fruit buds for the following year. So, not only is the crop light in the drought year, but in the next one too.

But on most fertile soils and in most years, there will be enough water in the soil to produce satisfactory growth. If trees and bushes are mulched annually with organic matter which eventually works down into the soil, there's nothing to worry about.

However, watering at the right time is most useful in increasing the size and weight of the harvested fruit. Experiments at East Malling have produced a remarkable fifty per cent increase in the weight of harvested fruit that had been watered. The time to apply it is just as the fruit is swelling. Once it starts to colour up, however, it's best to stop watering, which can at this stage damage the fruit and increase the chances of fungus diseases.

29 *A tall, tripod sprinkler will reach over the top of soft-fruit bushes*

Weed control

There's not a lot of point in expending time, energy and money on fertilisers and watering to feed a healthy crop of weeds. There aren't any morals in the world of nature, so they'll grab every bit of water and food they can without a thought for the poor old fruit trees. They must never be allowed to take hold.

The normal method of weed control is by hoeing and there's nothing wrong with that provided only the top half inch or so is disturbed (30). Fruit trees and particularly bushes are shallow-rooted, with most of their feeding roots very near the surface. Deep hoeing will do as much damage to the plants as the weeds would if they were left in.

An alternative to hoeing is to use a chemical weedkiller. One or at the most two sprays a year will generally be enough to keep the ground clean without disturbing the soil at all.

Some weedkillers for use amongst fruit are absorbed through the leaves of the weeds. They are not selective, so they will do as much damage to the cultivated plants if the chemical is allowed to touch their leaves. On bare bark or on the ground around the plants, they are perfectly safe. So, it is essential to ensure that none of the chemical touches the leaves of cultivated plants. If you are using a sprayer, work only on days when there's not a breath of wind and direct the sprayer right down at the base of the plants (31).

To get the best effect, the idea is to try to make the tiny droplets of weedkiller cling to the surface of the leaves. So, they don't need soaking. Indeed, once the spray starts to run off the leaf surface, the effect is lessened considerably. It's obviously better then to use a sprayer that will apply very small droplets rather than a watering-can where it's almost impossible to avoid putting on too much. The one exception

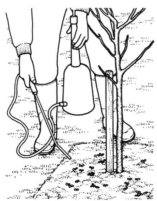

30 *Hoeing should be done at a very shallow depth to avoid root damage*

31 *Controlling weeds chemically is a sure way of avoiding root damage*

to this rule is where you are working in a very confined space. If it is at all difficult to avoid the fine spray drifting onto other plants, play safe and use a watering-can.

If you're going to do this, buy yourself a special one and either a fine rose or a weedkiller applicator. Paint 'Weedkiller' on the side in big red letters so that there's no chance of you using it by mistake for watering the tender young seedlings in your greenhouse.

If you decide to use weedkillers, read the labels carefully and abide strictly by the manufacturer's instructions. Never, never add an extra drop 'just for luck'. It could be the unluckiest thing you ever did. Keep all bottles in a place where the only person who can get at them is you, and never transfer weedkiller to another bottle. If you have some left, throw it away.

Finally, when you have finished spraying or watering, wash the can or sprayer out with plenty of clean water and a squirt of washing-up liquid *straight away*. Above all, even if the label on the bottle tells you that the weedkiller is harmless, get into the habit of treating all chemicals as if they were lethal. Give them the respect they deserve and they're as safe as houses.

Weedkillers

Paraquat-diquat (ICI Weedol). This is a contact weedkiller for annual weeds only. It acts on the chlorophyll-making mechanism of the leaves turning them yellow and eventually killing them. It can be used round all fruit trees and bushes except strawberries, provided care is taken to avoid splashing the leaves of cultivated plants. It can be used at any time of the year and is probably safest when the fruit is dormant, after the leaves have fallen.

Glyphosate (Murphy Tumbleweed). This chemical is taken in through the leaves and is then transported down to the roots of weeds. Here it prevents the roots storing food and so eventually kills both annuals and perennials. At least ten and preferably fourteen days should be allowed for the weedkiller to act before cultivating or removing the leaves. Again, it can be used on all fruit crops except strawberries.

Propachlor (Murphy Covershield). A useful weedkiller for controlling annual weeds in all fruit crops including strawberries. It is applied in granular form, so there is no risk of spray damage to nearby plants. It can be used at any time and its effects last for up to eight weeks.

There are, of course, other weedkillers which can be used in fruit crops, but these three have proved the most effective at Barnsdale and will cover most eventualities.

One problem which is difficult to solve is that of perennial weeds with underground storage roots which have become established in amongst the roots of an established fruit plot. Weeds like couch-grass or bindweed are extremely difficult to get rid of once they become established close to the plants. You can go on pulling it out from the branches of soft-fruit bushes till you're blue in the face, but still it comes back.

I solved the problem at Barnsdale by laboriously painting the shoots with a mixture of Tumbleweed and washing-up liquid. The weedkiller is mixed up as directed plus a squirt of washing-up liquid to help it to stick to the leaves. It is applied with an ordinary paint brush. A tedious and time-consuming task to be sure, but it certainly did the trick and there's only a need to do it once. I don't think I could have faced it again anyway.

Pests and diseases
Again, I'm afraid I dispute here most recommendations. While for many common pests like greenfly, the normal advice is to spray when the first insects are seen, I feel sure that the only really effective way is to use preventive sprays to get the little blighters before they have a chance to do any damage. Admittedly one or two greenfly won't eat a lot, but they are the common carriers of the dreaded virus diseases. Remember that there is no cure for virus. All you can do is to dig the plants up and burn them.

With this in mind, I have, under each separate heading, devised a routine spray programme which should, with luck, keep trees and bushes completely free from pests and diseases.

Bear in mind also, that there are some pests that are never seen until it's too late. One such culprit is codling moth which lays its eggs on the fruit in June or early July and the first you know of its existence is when you get a mouthful of maggot from an apple. Not a nice experience. Fungus diseases must also be controlled before they appear, since, though they can afterwards be controlled and prevented from spreading to some degree, they can't be eradicated. It seems sense then, while spraying against mildew, to include a greenfly killer and kill two birds with one stone.

To be really effective, pesticides should be applied with a pressure sprayer (32). They are not too expensive and will save you money in the long run. It is possible to buy many insecticides and fungicides in aerosols or puffer packs, but they are not as effective and will cost you an arm and a leg in the end.

Naturally, the same safety rules apply to insecticides and fungicides as were recommended for weedkillers.

32 *The best way to control pests on most fruits is with a regular spray programme*

5 APPLES

There's no fruit in the world to compare with an English apple and this deservedly puts them right at the top of the popularity poll. They can be eaten fresh from the tree or cooked, they will store until spring, they make decorative and highly productive trees and modern methods of growing make them ideal for even the smallest garden.

Modern research has been kind to us too. Naturally the scientific effort of government research stations is aimed primarily at the commercial grower but fortunately the results have produced new techniques which are ideally suited to the gardener too. Fruit farmers require small trees to avoid the time expended pruning and harvesting from ladders, they want their trees to come into full bearing as soon after planting as possible and to produce consistently big yields of high quality fruit. And for the same reasons of economy, they need a high degree of resistance to pests and diseases. Exactly up the gardener's alley, even though our reasons may be different.

Of course, research and advice aimed at the professional grower needs a large degree of adaptation to suit the gardener. Without the time, the expertise and the equipment of the commercial man, our methods must be simpler and less exacting. I honestly believe that many home gardeners are discouraged from fruit growing because of the sheer complication of the advice they receive. As in all specialised trades and professions, even the jargon takes a bit of understanding. So, the purists must forgive me if I simplify things somewhat. The methods I use at Barnsdale are aimed purely and simply at the gardener with limited space and without a degree in horticultural botany! I have attempted here, quite frankly, to make fruit growing as simple as possible.

Tree shapes

In my view, there are just three tree shapes worth considering for the gardener with limited space – cordons, espaliers and dwarf pyramids. All are designed with space-saving in mind, all will produce heavy crops and they are all very simple to prune.

Dwarf pyramids make attractive, free-standing bushes and can be planted as closely as 5ft (1.5m.) apart (33). Espaliers are ideal for growing against a wall or fence and make a very attractive decorative feature as well as producing lots of fruit in an otherwise unproductive space (34). Cordons can also be trained against a wall or fence, but are even better grown on a

33 *Dwarf pyramids make attractive, free-standing bushes*

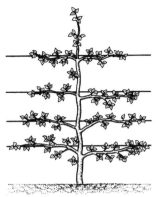

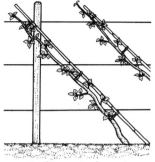

34 *Espaliers are ideal for growing against a fence or wall*

35 *Cordons trained on wires make an attractive hedge*

structure of posts and wires (35). Here they can be used as a very decorative hedge and are perhaps the most productive of all yard for yard of land used.

All these trees are pruned mainly in the summer, and there is a rule-of-thumb method that makes it almost impossible to go wrong. There is certainly no need to be put off fruit growing because of lack of space or because it appears complicated.

Choosing varieties

There are dozens and dozens of different varieties of apples and we all have our favourites. Most catalogues contain numerous different varieties, all described in glowing terms, making final selection a thought-provoking task. I have suggested the varieties I would prefer, but in the end, it must be a personal decision. There are really six main points to consider:

Pollination

No apple tree will set a full crop of fruit on its own pollen. The flowers of every variety need to be fertilised with the pollen of another variety in order to give the highest yields.

It's possible, of course, that your neighbour may have a couple of trees in his garden that flower at the same time as the varieties you choose, in which case you can grow just one tree. Indeed, if you are starting a garden on a new housing estate, you may be able to get together with your neighbour before buying apple trees to ensure that this is the case. But, if you're going to rely on your own trees to do the pollinating, it's essential to get two compatible trees at least.

Alas, there is a complication. Some varieties are incapable of pollinating anything at all so, if you want to grow one of these varieties, you'll need three trees. The top favourite cooker,

Bramley's Seedling, is one of these misfits which obstinately refuses to be monogamous. If you want to grow this, you'll need something like a Spartan to pollinate it and then a James Grieve perhaps to pollinate the Spartan.

Since there's not a better cooker anywhere than Bramley, most gardeners *will* want to grow it, so you can see why I suggest small trees.

The main criterion for good pollination is that trees flower at the same time, so make sure this is so before placing an order.

Having said that, if you have room for one ornamental tree, there is a good alternative. Flowering crab-apples will nearly all pollinate fruiting apple varieties. They flower over a long period and, of course, as ornamental trees they have been bred for an abundance of flower, which means in turn, an abundance of pollen. The best variety in my view, is *Malus 'Golden Hornet'* which, with its magnificent show of white flowers in spring followed by an abundance of bright yellow crab apples in the autumn makes an invaluable ornamental tree for a small garden. The apples could possibly be used for wine-making or jelly, though I must confess that I've never tried them.

Time of cropping

Obviously, the season can be extended considerably by choosing varieties that are ready for harvesting in succession.

For most of us I'm sure there is no better tasting apple than that first one that is picked and eaten straight from the tree each year, so most of us will want at least one early variety. But, bear in mind that early pickers don't store well. They will keep for no more than a few weeks and really need to be eaten fresh.

If you want to extend the season until well after Christmas, you'll also need a variety that matures late in the season and can be stored.

Use

Though dessert varieties can be cooked, they lack the flavour and texture of those varieties that were bred especially for the kitchen. If you don't have room for more than one tree, there are a few varieties that will serve both purposes. Frankly, I still think they're a bit of a compromise, so I'd always jolly well *make* room for at least one good cooker and a couple of eaters.

Cropping ability

In small gardens that can only support a couple of trees, we may as well face the fact that we'll never be able to produce enough fruit to see us through the whole season. Some will have to be bought, like it or not. So, to reduce the indignity of a visit to the greengrocer to a minimum, it seems sensible to grow as much as possible from the few trees we have. Sounds obvious I know, until you consider the most popular variety of them all. Cox's Orange Pippin may have a superb flavour, but it is such a poor cropper that it can only be recommended for the gardener with space to spare. I wouldn't give it garden room for that, and one other reason I'll explain later. Instead, I grow Suntan and I creep down to the greengrocer after dark for a pound or two of the undeniably flavoursome Cox.

Flavour

Many years ago in my long-distant youth, my guide and mentor at college once expressed the view that, if a grower painted a round piece of wood bright red and put it in the supermarket, not only would the average British housewife buy it as an apple, she'd come back for more! You only have to taste one of those floury, thick-skinned, insipid American Jonathan or the detestable French Golden Delicious to see his point. Both are best-sellers.

Though I do believe that growers are beginning to realise the importance of flavour, it's good looks that sell apples. The only answer for the more discerning is to grow your own.

Obviously, it's impossible to advise on such a matter of personal taste, but it may be worth visiting the nursery at harvest time and begging a bite of a sample apple before buying your trees. Why not?

Disease resistance

With the possible exception of virus diseases, the biggest scourge of apple trees without doubt is mildew. The white, powdery fungus that covers the growing tips of shoots affects all varieties of apples, stopping growth of young shoots dead.

It can be controlled by constant, regular spraying, but once it takes a hold it is impossible to eradicate that year and an even bigger threat the following year.

While all varieties are subject to attack, some are more resistant than others and conversely, some varieties are very prone. This then, is the second reason for my dislike of Cox's Orange Pippin.

To make matters worse, if you grow one mildew susceptible variety, it is likely to spread like wildfire to others.

So, in the same way that many rose-growers avoid these susceptible varieties, my list only contains those that will put up a good fight. I don't think that mildew resistance should be looked on as a reason not to spray, but it should certainly help avoid what can be a crippling disease. To ensure that you start with clean, virus-free stock, you should insist that, whatever the variety, it has a Ministry certificate to show that it's free from disease, shown by the initials EMLA on the label.

Time of flowering
In addition to my list of six points to consider when choosing varieties, I include one more important consideration for gardeners living towards the north of the country or in an area susceptible to late frosts. Here I would strongly recommend sticking to varieties that flower late. It could be the crucial factor between a good harvest and nothing at all.

Suggested varieties
To simplify the choice, I have selected six dessert varieties that have done well at Barnsdale and give a good continuity of cropping without overdue disease problems. With a couple of cookers, you should need no more. All will flower at roughly the same time to give good pollination throughout.

The late flowering list will also provide a succession of fruit and good pollination and these are to be preferred for gardeners living in the north.

Mid-season flowering

Discovery: undoubtedly the best early variety of them all. It is ready for picking in August/September and will keep a little longer than most earlies. The skin is pale greenish-yellow with a bright red flush and the flesh is crisp, juicy and delicious. It is rather more free than other varieties in dropping its fruit before it matures, so it is best left unthinned.

James Grieve: ready for picking from mid-September to October, this old variety is superb for gardeners. It is not so highly favoured by commercial fruit growers because it bruises easily and is at its best when eaten straight from the tree, but neither factor will worry gardeners. The skin is pale yellow with orange stripes and the flesh is very juicy and well flavoured. The flowers show some resistance to frost, so it's a good variety for northern gardeners.

Jupiter: a new variety from East Malling with all the attributes of Cox and none of its disadvantages. It will start to crop in late October when it is delicious eaten fresh and it will also store until well after Christmas. In trials, it consistently cropped three times more heavily than Cox.

Spartan: this is a fairly well-known variety because it has been grown and imported from America for some years. But, because of our more equable climate, it's much, much better for being grown in this country. The tough skin and floury centres typical of apples grown in the USA, disappear completely. Instead, the flesh is crisp and juicy and the very slightly acid flavour is excellent. It's a heavy cropper, ready for picking in early November and will keep until January. Again, the flowers show resistance to frost, so it's another good variety for the north of the country.

Kent: another new variety from East Malling, this was also a product of the programme aimed at producing a successor to Cox. It is ready for picking in November and will keep well into the new year. A heavy and regular cropper, the fruit has a dark red colour on a green background. The flesh is firm and juicy and the flavour pleasant. Though it flowers mid-season, it has been found that it will not cross-pollinate between Cox or Suntan, though the other suggested varieties are suitable.

Crispin: this one knocks those awful French Golden Delicious into a cocked hat. In colour it is much the same, but there the similarity ends. The fruit is larger, crisper, juicier and much better flavoured. It is somewhat prone to attack from apple scab disease and it will not pollinate other varieties. It is ready for picking in November and will keep well into February or even March.

Late flowering

Merton Charm: a relatively new variety which is ready for picking in September. The medium-sized, greenish-yellow fruit has a fine flavour and the flesh is crisp and juicy.

Orleans Reinette: a very old, French variety but still worth its place for its superb flavour and aroma. It crops in November and will keep for a month or so.

Ashmeads Kernel: an excellent old russet with incomparable flavour that deserves to be planted more widely. It is ready for picking in early December and will go on into March under good storage conditions.

Suntan: a fine new variety that improves no end in keeping. If you can keep your salivary glands under control until March, that's the time to eat it. Unfortunately, it will not pollinate other varieties.

Tydeman's Late Orange: a good storage variety that will last well into March given ideal conditions. The flesh is creamy and firm and the flavour excellent. It does tend to fall into the bad habit of cropping every other year if a very late frost prevents it fruiting one year.

Cooking varieties

Bramley's Seedling: certainly the most popular cooker and with good reason. The flavour and texture when cooked are unsurpassed and it crops regularly and heavily from October and will keep till March. It has two snags. Firstly, it will make a large tree and is therefore perhaps unsuitable for very small gardens and for growing as a cordon. At Barnsdale, I grow it as a dwarf pyramid without too much difficulty. It is also another awkward customer which won't pollinate other varieties. It flowers mid-season.

Grenadier: a good, old variety without the pollination problems of Bramley and not so vigorous. Flavour is good, though not quite so fine as a Bramley. It crops in August/September and flowers mid-season.

Howgate Wonder: if it's big cookers you're after, they don't come any bigger than this one. Flavour is fair only. It is a heavy cropper producing fruit ready for cooking in November. A good variety for northern gardens since it flowers late.

Lanes Prince Albert: another late flowering variety with perhaps a better flavour than Howgate Wonder. The flesh is soft, white and acid. It is ready for picking from November and will keep until March.

Rootstocks

It is not normal for apple trees to be grown on their own roots. If they were, the vigour of the trees would be very variable indeed. Varieties like the vigorous Bramley would grow into enormous giants, impossible to prune or to pick, while weak varieties would struggle all their lives.

Instead, the variety is budded onto a special rootstock which has been especially selected to control its vigour, and to encourage trees to start to bear fruit earlier in their lives.

Research into rootstocks is a continuous process and this has resulted in dozens of different ones, all having various and varied effects upon the growth of the trees. Much has been written about them – too much in my opinion. Frankly, the rootstock you use depends entirely on what the nurseryman has, and there simply isn't that much choice. So you can, in my view, happily forget the long and complicated lists of rootstocks and their different effects and simply concern yourself with the two that are commonly available. MM 106 is the stock commonly used for medium-sized trees on most soils. Growth will still vary a little depending on the fertility of your soil and the variety used, but generally the effect of the stock is to produce semi-dwarf trees which fruit early in their lives. As an example, Bramley's Seedling, one of the most vigorous trees you are likely to grow, will make a tree just a little higher than you can reach. Most of the picking and pruning will be possible from the ground, though you may eventually need to stand on short steps or a box to reach the very top.

M 9 is a dwarfing stock and is used for some trained trees and especially if you wish to grow apples in a large tub. The roots on this stock are likely to be a bit weak, so the trees will definitely need to be staked for the whole of their lives.

My own feeling is that, unless your soil is very fertile indeed, it's best to stick to MM 106 except for the special cases where very small trees are essential.

Planting

Follow the preparation and planting instructions detailed in Chapters 2 and 3. Remember that it is very important not to plant apple trees too deeply. The join between the variety and the rootstock, which is easily seen as a definite kink in the stem, must be well above the ground. If the rootstock is buried, the variety will take root and the advantage of the rootstock will be lost.

Plant dwarf pyramids 5ft (1.5m.) apart each way or, if you intend to grow more than one row, they can go 3½ft (1m.) apart in the row with 6ft (1.8m.) between the rows.

Cordons are planted 2½ft (75cm.) apart against a post and wire support, and this must be erected first. I used 3in. × 3in. (7.5cm. × 7.5cm.) cedar fencing posts 8ft (2.5m.) long and 10ft (3m.) apart. On my light land, I found it essential to concrete the posts 2ft (60cm.) into the ground. On different soil, you may get away with a couple of bricks rammed in to prevent movement when the wires are tightened. These should be strained tightly between the posts with the first one about 2ft (60cm.) from the ground, one at the top and one in the middle.

It's not a good idea to tie the trees directly to the wires because the support will be minimal and there is bound to be some chafing of the bark. A better bet is to tie them to bamboo canes which are in turn tied to the wires. Use 8ft (2.5m.) canes set at an angle of 45 degrees and fixed to the wires with either strong nylon string or galvanised wire.

Ideally, the tops of the canes should face north, though in small gardens this is often impossible. Bear it in mind though

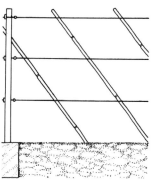

36 *A support for cordon apples*

and face them as near that way as possible, since this will give slightly more even growth.

Espaliers are generally trained against a fence or wall, though there's no reason at all why they shouldn't be grown against wires too.

If you're buying trees that are already shaped, the position of the existing horizontal branches will determine the height of the wires. If you're braver and intend to train your own from scratch, the wires should be round about 1ft (30cm.) apart. Espaliers make quite large trees, so allow at least 12ft (3.5m.) and preferably 15ft (4.5m.) between trees. Again, the branches are tied to canes fixed to the wires.

Feeding

Feeding of apple trees can be as easy or as complicated as you wish to make it. Certainly, the commercial fruit farmer would wish to be very precise. If you're talking about a thousand trees, the cost of fertiliser would be astronomic and no one who is looking to make a profit from his trees would dream of shovelling it on ad lib. There is no doubt either, that accurate fertiliser application can make a difference to the final crop. If you're making your living out of it, that crop needs to be a hundred per cent.

But gardeners have no need to be so concerned about accuracy. With only half-a-dozen trees, the cost of a little wastage can be measured in pence rather than pounds, and we would hardly notice the difference between a ninety-five and a hundred per cent crop. In my experience, if we make it too complicated we simply never do it at all, with the result that the final yield is reduced significantly.

With this in mind, I have, over the past few years, been experimenting with compound fertilisers which will supply all the plants' needs in one application. I can honestly say that I have noticed no drop in yields or reduction in growth. In fact, the reverse is the case, no doubt because, with a simple method which takes only a few minutes, the trees get fed at the right time and at more or less the right rate.

I use an organic fertiliser because I believe that over-application has somewhat less harmful side-effects on the plants and the soil population.

In the first year after planting, there is no need to feed at all. The initial planting fertiliser plus the organic matter worked into the soil will supply all the plants' needs.

In subsequent years, they should be fed in late February or early March, using blood, fish and bone fertiliser at 3oz. per sq. yd (90gm per sq. m.). Apply as suggested in Chapter 4.

If the trees are growing in grass, the fertiliser must be applied earlier in February so that it has a chance of reaching the root zone before the grass starts into active growth.

As I have pointed out earlier, all plants need other elements in tiny quantities, which can be supplied by an annual mulch of organic matter.

Thinning

It's not easy to bring yourself to remove your hard-won fruit long before it has matured enough to be usable. But in some cases and in some years it is vital.

In a good year, when there have been no late frosts to damage blossom and conditions for pollination have been good, trees can produce vast numbers of fruits. Some of these they will shed naturally, but this will still often leave far more than the tree can happily cope with. If they're left on, they will inevitably be small. While I appreciate that most families actually prefer fruit that is not over-large, very small apples tend to be less juicy and lacking in flavour.

But much worse than this is the fact that an over-large crop can have a serious effect on next year's yield. So much energy is spent in 'breast-feeding' the offspring, that poor old Mum needs a rest. To make matters worse, an over-good year followed by a rest can, in some varieties, be habit forming and, for the rest of its life, that tree may bear fruit only once every other year.

And there's no need to worry about losing fruit by thinning. In fact, because the fruit is larger, the overall *weight* of the crop will be no smaller and often even bigger than it would have been had the trees been left unthinned.

The timing of the operation is crucial. Apples will naturally drop a proportion of their fruit every year so it's best to wait until after this has happened. The phenomenon is known in informed circles as, 'The June Drop'. Don't ask me why because at Barnsdale it has never occurred before July and I believe this to be so in most parts of the country.

Anyway, whenever it happens you certainly won't miss it. You'll walk out one morning to the accompaniment of a great crunching underfoot and there will be dozens of small apples on the ground. That's the time to start thinning.

The amount to remove depends upon the variety and the size of fruit you are aiming for. With most dessert varieties, it should be sufficient to thin each cluster to leave the fruits about 4in. (10cm.) apart. Larger cooking apples, especially those like Howgate Wonder, need only one fruit remaining on each cluster.

37 *Thin out misshapen fruits and the largest in the cluster first*

They can generally be twisted off, but if you have difficulties, snip them off with a pair of sharp-pointed scissors.

Start by removing any fruitlets that are badly misshapen. Then look at the centre of the cluster and remove the biggest apple and after that take away any that are overcrowded (37).

Support

Having read this book, you can, of course, look forward to massive crops! A heavy crop of apples is going to put quite a strain on the branches and it's important to avoid breakages. Some bending down of branches is desirable, because it tends to flatten them out permanently thus actually strengthening the joint between branch and trunk. Obviously though, if the weight is excessive there is a risk that the branch may break. So, towards the end of the season, when the branches are beginning to groan, it's advisable to give them some support. You can do this by propping them up with a forked stick or by tying the branch to another higher up, or to the trunk, with strong nylon string. If you do use string though, it's as well to wrap a bit of sacking around both branches to avoid chafing the bark.

Pruning

Of all factors likely to put gardeners off growing fruit entirely, I'm sure that the complexity of pruning is the biggest culprit. Faced with the mind-boggling alternatives of 'The Open Centre' system, 'Renewal Pruning', 'The Delayed Open Centre' method, etc., I don't blame anyone for giving up in despair. So, I made the simplification of pruning a top priority exercise at Barnsdale.

I was looking for just one simple method and eventually settled for three. The reason, of course, for three methods is that they produce three differently shaped trees, each with its own purpose. If you want a free-standing tree, go for a dwarf pyramid; if it's a hedge you're after, perhaps to divide the ornamental garden from the vegetable plot, use cordons, while if you have a wall to cover, an espalier is the best bet.

In fact, all methods are simple to follow and can, in the main, be done in the summer. There are one or two basic rules that should be followed whatever system you use.

First of all, you'll need a pair of sharp secateurs. Which type you use matters not at all, but do make sure they are kept very sharp.

When you prune, always cut back to just above a bud (38). Otherwise the stub left will die back and may introduce disease. Remember that the bud will grow out in the direction

38 *When pruning, always use sharp secateurs and cut back to a bud*

it's facing, so it is normal to cut back to an outward-facing bud to avoid branches growing into the tree and causing congestion. If you are cutting a branch out altogether, cut it right back to the point where it joins the tree.

After pruning, always pick up the prunings and burn them. Here lies another source of disease.

Dwarf pyramids: the final shape of a tree you are aiming for is rather like a Christmas tree. There is a centre stem with branches longer at the bottom than at the top.

If you have bought a 'maiden' tree with only one centre stem and no side-branches, prune it after planting by cutting back to a good bud to leave the stem about 2ft (60cm.) long (39).

This job can be done any time between November and March and is all that is necessary in the first year.

In the second year or if you have bought a tree with side-branches, you can start the initial shaping of the tree. Again, this phase is done in the winter.

Start by looking at the lower branches. Select a tier of about five or six branches that have a fairly wide angle with the main stem and are evenly spaced around it like the spokes of a wheel. Cut these back to an outward or downward-facing bud to leave them about 10in. (25cm.) long. If they are less than 10in. (25cm.) long, simply remove about 1in. (2.5cm.) from the tip. Extra branches should be completely removed (40).

Now progress to the upper branches for the next tier. Again, select five or six and this time cut them back to leave 6in. (15cm.).

The tip of the main stem is also cut back at this time to leave it about 12in. (30cm.) above the uppermost branch.

That's all the winter pruning you'll have to do, and if you think that's simple, wait till you get to the summer pruning.

From now on, all but the main stem are pruned in the summer. The best time to do this is the beginning of August to avoid the buds growing out again the same year.

This time, look at each side-branch separately. It will be easy to see the current year's growth, recognised by its lighter colour and softer wood. You can also see where you pruned last time. It is this new growth that is pruned each year.

Cut the tip of the branch to leave 6in. (15cm.) of this year's growth. If there are any side-branches from this branch, cut back to leave 4in. (10cm.) of new growth. If there are any shoots arising from the side-shoots, cut those back to 2in. (5cm.). Treat all the branches in the same way, and then turn your attention to any new branches growing out of the main stem. They should be cut back to leave 6in. (15cm.) of new

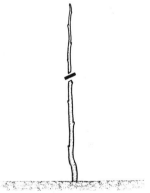

39 *Dwarf pyramid maidens with no 'feathers' are cut back to leave about 2ft after planting*

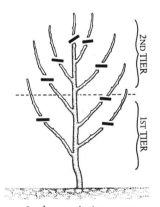

40 *In the second winter, prune the lower branches to 10in. and the upper ones to 6in. The leading shoot is cut back to leave 12in.*

41 *In the summer, cut back the branches to 6in., the side shoots to 4in. and the sub-side-shoots to 2in. Leave the leading shoot alone*

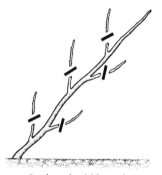

42 *Cordons should have their side-shoots taken back to 3in. after planting. Thereafter, prune in the summer*

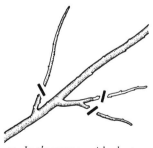

43 *In the summer, side-shoots arising from the main stem are cut back to 3in. and any shoots coming from them to 1in.*

growth. Again, if there are any shoots less than the required length, prune them back by 1in. (2.5cm.). So, all you have to remember is: Branches 6in., side-shoots 4in. and sub-side-shoots 2in. Leave the main stem unpruned (41).

As you may have expected, there is one complication. Some varieties bear their fruit right on the tips of branches. Obviously, a pruning system that cuts off all the tips also cuts off all the fruit on those branches. So, we reach a compromise. Any new shoots that are less than 6in. (15cm.) long are left unpruned and it is these that will bear fruit. In my list, the only varieties that need to be treated like this are Discovery and Bramley though in my experience, both will produce fruit even if they are tip-pruned.

In the winter, the only pruning left to do is to cut back the main stem to leave about 8in. (20cm.) of the current season's growth.

In subsequent years, the same procedure is repeated until the tree begins to fill its space and to get too high. Then, be more drastic with summer pruning, cutting back twice as hard, i.e. branches 3in., side-shoots 2in. and sub-side-shoots 1in.

When you can no longer reach the top of the main stem, cut this back in the summer too, treating it just like another branch.

Cordons: pruning cordons is even easier. Immediately after planting in the winter, prune any side-shoots there may be to 3in. (7.5cm.) cutting back to a downward-pointing bud. From then on, all pruning is done in the summer (42). Again, summer pruning is done in early August. The idea here, is to build up a cluster of very short branches called 'spurs' all up the stem. New shoots arising straight from the main stem are cut back to 3in. (7.5cm.). Any shoots arising from these are cut back to 1in. (2.5cm.) (43). Leave the main stem unpruned. And that's all there is to it.

In subsequent summers, simply repeat the operation. When the tree reaches the top of the cane, untie it and drop it about 10 degrees, tie another length of cane to the first and allow the tree to grow on. When it eventually reaches the end of the second cane, treat the main stem like a new spur, cutting back to leave 3in. (7.5cm.) of the new growth.

Espaliers: here you need to first produce about three to five side branches 12in. (30cm.) apart which are trained horizontally along wires. These branches are treated exactly as if they were cordons.

As I have suggested, you can buy trees that already have the three or five branches trained. But it's much more exciting to

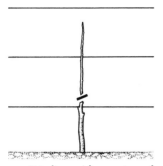
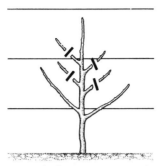
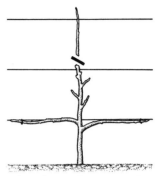

44 *Espalier maidens are pruned about 2in. above the first wire immediately after planting*

45 *In the first summer, train the two side-branches at 45 degrees and the centre branch straight up. Prune side-shoots to 3in.*

46 *In the second winter, tie the first tier of side-shoots down to the wires and prune the main stem to 2in. above the second wire. Afterwards, prune like cordons*

do it yourself and not at all difficult.

If you start with a 'maiden' with no side-branches, prune it to about 2in. (5cm.) above the first wire (44). What you are looking for are three good buds. The top one will grow straight up to form the main stem, while the other two will form the side-branches. Ideally those bottom two should face right and left.

If you start with a tree that has two well-placed side-branches already, they can be used as the first tier of branches. Cut them back by about a third.

As the side-branches grow during the first year, the top one should be tied in to a cane to grow straight up. The other two are also tied to canes but these should be tied to the wires at about 45 degrees from the main stem. If they are tied down horizontally too soon, growth will be restricted. They can be tied into their final positions at the end of the first season.

In that first summer, any side-shoots coming either from the main stem or from the side-branches should be treated just like cordons, cutting back to 3in. (7.5cm.) (45).

In the second winter, repeat the process, cutting the main stem back to 2in. (5cm.) above the second wire and selecting the three buds for the second tier (46). The side-branches can be left unpruned unless growth has been weak. In this case, pruning back by about a third of the new growth will stimulate them into fresh effort next year.

When all the tiers have been formed and the tree reaches the top wire, select just two buds instead of three and train these horizontally. Summer pruning is all that is then necessary and this is just a matter of cutting back side-shoots to 3in. (7.5cm.) and sub-side-shoots to 1in. (2.5cm.).

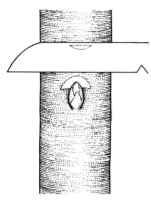

47 *To encourage growth, nick out a small piece of bark just above the bud*

Nicking and notching

Sometimes a trained tree will stubbornly refuse to produce branches in a particular part of the stem, resulting in long, bare areas which never bear spurs or fruit. It is possible to encourage any particular growth bud you want to grow away, and so shape the tree just as you want it.

All trees have a system by which they ensure that the top bud grows more strongly than those below. Thus, in forest conditions they are able to reach up for the light. They do it by sending a growth inhibiting substance down from the top of the tree to each bud in turn. The channels for transporting this material are just below the bark, so all that is needed is to cut them off before they get to the bud you wish to encourage.

Just make a very small nick above the bud and the inhibitor will miss that one, allowing it to grow away (47). The time to do it is May. Conversely, the inhibitor can be concentrated around the bud by cutting a notch below it to prevent it growing out.

Harvesting and storing

Early varieties are best picked just a little before they are fully ripe. They tend to go a bit mealy if left on the tree. Test for ripeness by gently lifting the fruit. If it parts easily from the tree, it's ready for picking. If not, leave it for a day or two. Later varieties should be left on as long as possible. They'll store better that way.

The fruits that are most exposed to the sun are naturally ready first. These are generally near the top of the tree, followed by those on the outside and lastly by the fruits inside the leaf canopy where they are more shaded. Always pick very carefully to avoid bruising and put, never throw, the fruit into a basket lined with soft cloth.

Storage varieties must be carefully looked over after picking. Take them into a cool room and lay them out so that they can dry right off and breathe for a day or two. Remove any that are bruised, damaged or attacked by pests or disease. They should all be used straight away. Then carefully pack one variety at a time into separate polythene bags and seal the tops. It's essential that the fruit should have air, so prick a few holes in the top of the bag before storing in a cool, dry, frost-free place. As a rough guide, prick two pin-holes for every 2lb (1kg.) of fruit. Generally the garage is ideal, though on frosty nights you may have to take extra frost precautions.

Check over the bags regularly. If you don't have too many in each, you should be able to see any fruits that look as though they're going off. They must be removed and used immediately or they'll quickly affect the rest.

Pests and diseases

The best way to control pests and diseases is by the use of a regular spray programme. However, this doesn't mean starting at the beginning of the year with a lethal cocktail which will kill all forms of life and going on until the winter. Indeed, such a programme could make matters worse by killing all the insects that live on the pests.

It's important though, to keep a very keen eye open for some pests and diseases and to apply a preventive spray for others which you can't see until it's too late.

Green cluster

Time of spraying depends entirely on the stage of growth of the tree, so rather than give dates, which would differ with variety and locality, I have used terms which relate to the stage of growth of the buds, blossom and fruit. They are clearly illustrated here (48).

In order to cut down the number of sprays I have to apply, I have used one manufacturer's products so that I can mix them together. It's never a good idea to mix two chemicals unless the manufacturer specifically recommends it. By using a mixture of permethrin (ICI Picket) and the fungicides triforine and bupirimate contained in ICI Nimrod 'T', it's possible to control quite a wide range of pests and diseases. There are others, of course, which need special treatment but it's possible to wait until you see these and then to buy the extra chemicals.

Pink bud

The mixture should be sprayed on at the green cluster stage, the pink bud stage, at petal fall and twice more in mid-June and early July. The pests and diseases controlled are listed below together with the symptoms of attack.

Aphids: generally seen as small insects clustered round tips of shoots and buds.

Apple sawfly: cause scars on fruits and large messy holes where the grubs have come out of the fruit.

Petal fall

48 *Stages of blossom development*

Codling moth: rarely seen before it is too late. The grubs are found inside harvested apples and leave small holes in the fruit.

Tortrix moth: attacks show as marks of nibbling on the fruits.

Winter moth: these caterpillars burrow into buds and later feed on blossom and leaves which are loosely spun together.

Apple scab: causes dark, sooty spots on leaves and fruit.

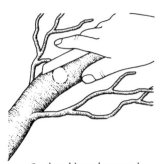

49 *Cankered branches must be cut back to healthy wood. Pare the wound clean and paint*

Mildew: shows as a white, powdery coating on shoots, leaves and flower trusses. The shoots have a silvery appearance in winter.

The mixture suggested will control the major pests and diseases. If you see symptoms of other pests and diseases listed below, spray them as suggested immediately.

Woolly aphid: forms greyish, woolly clusters on the branches and trunks of trees, often around pruning wounds. Spray with dimethoate (Murphy Systemic Insecticide).

Red spider mite: clusters of tiny red mites causing a bronzing of the leaves. Spray with pirimiphos methyl (ICI Sybol 2).

Canker: causes rough, granular or sunken wounds and die-back of branches. Cut out dead wood back to healthy tissue and paint with a fungicidal paint (PBI Arbrex) (49).

Brown rot: the cause of rotting fruit on the tree. Spray with Benomyl (PBI Benlate) 3–4 weeks before harvest. If infection is not severe, remove and burn affected fruit.

6 PEARS

Pears are not nearly as popular as apples and it must be admitted that they do have their problems. They are not as easy to grow, they are less vigorous in growth, they flower earlier and are therefore subject to late spring frosts and the fruits will keep for only a short time.

Nonetheless, no gardener should be put off growing them unless the problems of frost make it impossible. The difference between a well-ripened, home-grown pear and those tough old chaps you buy from the greengrocer make them well worth the extra trouble.

Growing pears is very much akin to growing apples so, with a few subtle variations, you simply have to follow the advice given in the previous chapter. However, if you have the choice, plant your pears in the warmest spot in the garden. Even in the north of the country, they will succeed well on a south-facing wall grown as an espalier or as cordons.

Tree shapes
Once again, I'm going to stick to my three favourite tree shapes for the small garden.

They are rather more upright growing than apples, so they make excellent dwarf pyramids and it's certainly worth including a couple on the end of a row of cordon apples.

Choosing varieties
Like apples, pears must be considered self-sterile. All varieties need another variety to pollinate them. Some nurserymen advertise the variety Conference as self-fertile, and this is true to a degree. However, pollinated with its own pollen, the fruit will be long, thin and badly shaped, the flavour not a patch on that of a cross-pollinated pear and the yield will be considerably lower.

In my first years at Barnsdale, I deliberately grew Conference on its own. The result was a few pears that looked more like cucumbers with a slight swelling on one end. After planting a pollinator, the difference was instant and very marked. Believe me, it's not worth growing them on their own.

Once again, you'll need varieties that flower at the same time and there are some that are incompatible. However, these are easily avoided if you only want to grow a few.

Time of harvesting is probably an even more important consideration than with apples. Pears will not keep nearly as long and are, in my view, much better eaten soon after picking. So, a succession of harvesting is very valuable in prolonging the season.

Cropping ability is perhaps less important. Pears will not give the same weight of fruit as apples and there is not nearly such a marked difference between varieties.

Again, I have given two lists of varieties, one early flowering and the other later. Bearing in mind the naturally earlier flowering of all pears, it is perhaps even more important to plant the second list in northern areas or where there is a record of late spring frosts.

Early flowering

Conference: certainly one of the most popular varieties, mainly because of its record of heavy cropping and the fact that it will store better than most. It will, in fact keep until well after Christmas if it's possible to regulate the storage temperature between 32 and 34°F, but this is a tall order for the gardener. A good indication though, that the lower the temperature above freezing, the better.

A green pear, it changes to greenish yellow with age and the flavour is sweet and juicy. It is ready for picking from the middle of October through November.

Williams Bon Chrétien: the best known and widest-planted pear of them all, Williams is ready for picking early in September and has a characteristic musky flavour. It is very juicy with white, melting flesh. Unfortunately, it has a short harvesting season and it will not keep well.

Beth: a brand new variety from East Malling, this one looks like a winner all the way. It's an early maturing variety of excellent texture and flavour, not unlike Williams. The fruit tends to be a bit on the small side if it's left unthinned, but it keeps better than Williams so could be a good substitute.

Merton Pride: a newish variety, which seems to be quite an event with pears. It is a regular, though not a heavy cropper, producing firm, juicy fruit of excellent flavour. It's ready for picking during late September. This is one of the few awkward customers that won't pollinate other varieties, so three trees are needed if you want to grow it.

Late flowering

Gorham: a pretty good cropper with a relatively long harvesting period. The juicy, fairly well-flavoured fruit is ready from the middle of September. It's perhaps best picked a little early and ripened off the tree.

Onward: yet another newish variety, this one is noted for heavy, regular crops, of very fair quality fruit. Its one disadvantage is that it doesn't keep very long, but the flavour is good so you probably won't be able to anyway.

Doyenné du Comice: the best-flavoured variety of them all. It's ready for picking in late October and goes on through November. Flavour and texture are unequalled. It needs a fairly sheltered spot for best results and it's at its best on a south wall.

Rootstocks

Just like apples, pears are also budded onto a special rootstock in order to control vigour and bring the trees into bearing earlier in their lives. There are, however, just two rootstocks commonly in use, so choice is fairly easy this time. Quince A is probably the most common stock in use. It produces fairly vigorous trees but, since with pears there is none of the rampant growth of apples, the trees are unlikely to become unmanageable. Certainly it is to be preferred on poor soils.

Quince C is a more dwarfing stock which induces trees to fruit earlier on in their lives as well as keeping them smaller. If there is a choice, use this one for cordons and for the rather more vigorous variety Doyenné du Comice as a dwarf pyramid.

Some varieties are incompatible with Quince rootstocks, so the growers graft another variety onto the stock, and then the incompatible variety onto that. The most common 'renegades' are Williams and Merton Pride. Don't worry if you can't see the extra piece of wood grafted on when you buy your trees. Nurserymen sometimes use a very cunning method of double budding instead of grafting, and it's almost undetectable.

Planting and pruning

Planting is exactly the same as described for apples except that, since the habit of growth is generally more upright, dwarf-pyramid trees can be planted somewhat closer. They can go as close as 3½ft (1m.) apart in the row, but if you are growing more than one row, it's as well to leave 7ft (2m.) between the rows to make spraying and cultivations easier.

There is no difference in pruning methods except that pears can be started earlier than apples. I normally start the tree-fruit pruning year with the pears round about the middle of July.

Cultivations

The year's work is almost identical to the apple calendar. Feeding is more or less the same except that, since pears relish a little more nitrogen than apples, the annual mulch with manure or compost is more important.

Thinning, in my experience is rarely necessary. It needs a very good pear year to make me thin. However, it does happen from time to time and when I get a very heavy crop, I thin to two fruits per cluster.

Harvesting and storing

To get pears really at their best requires a bit of vigilance, perhaps a year or two of experience and I suppose a certain amount of luck. As with apples, early varieties are treated somewhat differently to the later ones.

The earlies, like Williams and Merton Pride, are best picked early when they are still green and hard. Personally, I like a hard pear, so I pick them and eat them more or less straight from the tree. If you have more refined taste than I, you may well want to allow them to develop that softer, melting flesh that insists on dribbling rivulets of juice down your chin.

To get them to that stage, they must first be picked just when they part easily from the tree when lifted and slightly twisted. Place them on a shelf, just as they are, without wrapping, in the coldest spot you can find. It's unlikely, at that time of year that there will be frost enough to harm them if they're in the garage or shed, but if there is any danger of the temperature falling that low, they must be protected.

Don't be misled into thinking that they are defying the laws of Nature and remaining in good condition for some time. This often appears to be the case, because they will stay hard and green on the outside. Left too long though, the inside can go soft and mushy and develop that characteristic metallic taste. I would reckon that early varieties, even under ideal storage conditions will keep for no more than a couple of weeks at the outside.

To get them to ripen evenly and perfectly, they need slightly higher temperatures, so you need to plan ahead. Bring them into the living room about two days before you want to eat them, and they'll ripen perfectly.

Even later varieties will not keep too long. With these, it's best to leave them on the tree for as long as possible, though they must not be allowed to ripen fully on the trees. Inspect the trees as often as you can at the end of the season and, as soon as they will part from the tree easily with a lift and a twist, they should be picked and stored.

Storage is just the same for late varieties but again, don't expect them to keep too long.

Of course, though pears will not keep long fresh, do remember that they can be preserved in other ways. While they don't freeze too well, there can be no better fruit for bottling, especially the varieties Doyenné du Comice and Williams.

Pests and diseases

Pears are subject to much the same pests and diseases as apples and they can be controlled with the same spray programme. Bear in mind that, since pears flower earlier than apples, the bud and blossom stages illustrated for apples will occur a little earlier. The only other difference is the obvious one that the blossoms are white, so if you wait for the 'pink-bud' stage, you'll wait forever. The emerging petals look exactly the same except that they are, of course, white.

There are a couple of extra pests of pears, one of which will be controlled by the spray programme. The other certainly won't and you should be on the lookout for it.

Pear sucker: this causes a sticky, honeydew excretion on leaves and blossoms. Generally a sooty mould grows on the honeydew. The recommended spray programme will control it.

Fireblight: this one is a real killer and demands immediate action. The culprit is a bacterium which causes wilting of the fruit trusses or shoot tips, initially. It then travels through the tree causing the leaves to turn red/brown and to die.

The reddish coloration of the tree is impossible to mistake and is the reason for the highly descriptive name of the disease.

Alas, there is no weapon in the armoury to kill the bacterium. All that can be done is to cut out the infected wood to healthy tissue and burn it. But, such problems has it caused amongst professional growers, that it has been classed as a notifiable disease. If you even suspect that a tree may be infected, you should contact your local Ministry of Agriculture office. You'll find them in the 'phone book under 'Agriculture'. They'll send a man out who'll tell you what to do. Bear in mind too, that it can also affect other trees and shrubs in your garden, so it's in your own interest to get it seen to straight away.

Growing apples and pears in tubs

However small your garden, you can still grow apples and pears. Indeed, it's possible even if you have no garden at all, since they will grow quite happily in a large tub.

Obviously, the larger the tub the better. I have grown trees for many years in a couple of sawn-off beer barrels about three feet across and they have fruited very well indeed.

Naturally, a dwarfing rootstock is essential, and they are better off in a sheltered spot, since the anchorage is somewhat suspect and they are difficult to stake.

For apples, choose trees on a Malling 9 or the newer and even dwarfer Malling 27 rootstock. Pears should be budded on to Quince c.

When potting, make sure first of all that there is ample drainage through the tub. I think it's essential to raise it slightly off the ground so that water can drain freely out and to ensure a good circulation of air. There should be plenty of large holes in the bottom of the tub, and these are best covered with a bit of broken pot or similar concave object to prevent soil blocking the holes while still allowing water through.

Put a couple of inches of coarse stones in the bottom and cover these with some fibrous material. I use a forkful of well-rotted manure but garden compost is as good.

Use a soil-based potting compost, rather than a soil-less one. Bear in mind that, in the best regulated gardens, tubs and troughs do tend to get forgotten sometimes, and the soil will provide a good 'buffer' against drying out if you neglect the watering. John Innes Potting Compost No. 3 is ideal.

Plant as you would normally, with the joint between rootstock and variety well above soil-level, and leave the compost a couple of inches below the top of the pot to allow for watering.

Pruning is carried out in exactly the same way as trees grown in the garden and there is no doubt that dwarf pyramids are the ideal shape for pot-growing. If you have a wall or fence with a concrete or paving path right next to it and you want to cover it, *don't* try growing an espalier or a fan in a pot. They make much bigger trees and need a lot more than the tub could provide. Much better roll up your shirtsleeves and bash a hole in the concrete.

Feeding and watering are entirely your responsibility and you can expect no help from the Met. Office. However much it rains, you will still have to supplement the water in the spring and summer. In the winter, when the trees have no leaves, they'll look after themselves. Bear in mind also, that the only food they'll be able to get after the initial supply runs out, must come from you too. I use a solid fertiliser – blood, fish and bone again – putting on a couple of handfuls in February and repeating the dose in June. I also top up the tub with well-rotted manure in the winter after picking.

Keep a close eye on the trees and if they show any signs of leaf discoloration, spray them with a foliar feed like PBI Fillip, and give them a liquid fertiliser at the same time.

In the winter, there is a tendency for tubs to freeze solid and this does the roots no good at all. So, when the weather turns really cold, it pays to give them a treat by wrapping the tub with a couple of sacks or a good insulating layer of straw. There's nothing, as you know, that makes you feel more comfortable than nice warm feet.

Family trees
If your garden is really small, leaving room for only one or two trees, you can treble the variety and spread the harvesting period by growing family trees. These are apple or pear trees on which three or sometimes even four varieties are budded onto the same rootstock.

The varieties are carefully selected so that they are all of much the same sort of vigour, so that one doesn't eventually take over. This is still a bit of a problem, however careful the grower may be, but you can expect to get at least ten years or more out of the tree before this happens.

Many specialist growers now stock family trees and there is quite a reasonable selection of varieties.

7 PLUMS

Because of their size, plums are not the most popular trees in modern gardens. Like cherries, they also suffer from severe bird damage and those enormous old trees are quite impossible to net. But, there are ways of growing plums in small gardens, especially now that a dwarfing rootstock has been developed, so it looks as though this delicious fruit could well be destined for a comeback. There's no doubt that plums present more problems to gardeners than most tree fruits but, if these can be overcome, the fruits are delicious and well worth growing.

Tree shapes

For the small garden, there are only two tree shapes worth considering. If it's a free-standing tree you're after, they make excellent dwarf pyramids which, even on one of the traditional rootstocks, can be controlled by pruning to keep them to a reasonable size. They will really need to be protected from birds which can strip the young fruit buds at an alarming rate, so the best spot for them is within the fruit cage.

Bullfinches are the chief culprits and, if they are a problem in your area and you don't possess a fruit cage, you will have to resort to winding cotton in and out of the branches, which seems to be a fairly successful deterrent.

Much easier to protect from birds are plums grown as fans. They do extremely well on a south or west-facing wall and they'll fruit quite satisfactorily on even a northerly aspect, but the fruit will be a little later. It's but a minor feat of engineering to rig up a protection of netting over a fan-trained tree.

One other problem should be considered when thinking about tree shapes. Plums suffer badly from a disease known as silver leaf. The fungus that causes it enters through wounds or pruning cuts, and this is most likely to occur during the period from September to March. If pruning can be restricted to the summer, as is the case with dwarf pyramids and fans, the risk of infection is much reduced.

Varieties

Plums flower in April when there is still a risk of frost so, if you live in an area prone to late frosts, choose a late-flowering variety. However, the flowering period extends only for about three weeks, whatever the variety you choose, so northern gardeners may not find plums a realistic proposition.

Pollination is another factor that has to be considered, but they are much more accommodating than apples or pears.

Some varieties are fully self-fertile, so it's quite possible to grow just one tree. The varieties I have chosen here are all self-fertile.

Denniston's Superb: an early variety with a sweet, pleasant flavour. It has the one disadvantage that it flowers early. The fruits are green with a red flush.

Czar: a good all-round plum in my view, although it is often catalogued as a cooker. I certainly eat it fresh from the tree and always come back for more. It crops in early August and flowers late. It shows some frost resistance and at Barnsdale is one of the most reliable of varieties. It produces large purple fruits with a slightly acid flavour.

Victoria: the most popular of all plums and with good reason. It flowers mid-season and crops in late August to September. The fruits are large, deep red, juicy and well flavoured. They are equally good eaten fresh or cooked and this is the heaviest cropping variety of them all. Add to that the fact that it is self-fertile and you can see that it fully deserves its spot at the top of the charts. It does have the one disadvantage that it is rather more susceptible to silver leaf disease than most other varieties but, if pruning is always done in the summer, that shouldn't put you off.

Marjorie's Seedling: a late flowerer that may well miss the late frosts. It is ready for picking in late September or early October and hangs on the tree for some time after it is ripe. The fruits are large and deep blue and, though again often classed as a cooker, the flavour in my view is good enough to eat fresh. It crops well and regularly.

Rootstocks

There are really only two rootstocks available that are suitable for small trees. Trees grown on Brompton or Myrobalan stocks make enormous trees quite unsuitable for small spaces.

I don't think many nurserymen supplying home gardeners, use either of these now, but it's worth asking just in case. I'd avoid them like the plague unless you've got a couple of acres to play with.

St Julien A, is a semi-dwarfing stock and is very suitable for growing dwarf pyramids in small gardens.

Pixy is a new stock from East Malling and is the first really dwarfing stock for plums. It will produce trees about half the normal size and it comes into cropping earlier. The root system is weak so it will need staking all its life and is not suitable for poor soils. An ideal stock for both dwarf pyramids and fans.

Planting

Though, like all fruit trees, plums demand good drainage, they will not do well unless the soil is capable of retaining water. For this reason they are eminently suitable for heavy soils.

On all soils, especially the lighter ones, it's well worth preparing the land well by deep digging and the addition of plenty of organic matter.

Plant in the normal way, setting dwarf pyramids 10ft (3m.) apart on Julien A stocks and 6ft (1.8m.) apart on Pixy. If you intend to grow two fan-trained trees, put them at least 12ft (3.5m.) apart.

Because of the risk of silver leaf infection, great care must be taken with staking. If the bark of the tree is allowed to rub against the stake, it will almost certainly fracture, leaving an inviting entrance for the fungus. So, use a short stake for free-standing trees and cut off the bottom branches so that there is no chance of them rubbing on the stake. Always use a proper tree-tie with a collar that ensures that the tree is held slightly away from the stake. After about five years, when the trees have made sufficient roots, the stakes should be removed completely.

When buying trees, again it's worth going to a specialist grower. Ask for trees with the EMLA label to ensure a virus-free start. The same criteria for dwarf pyramid apples apply to plums, but for fans, there are two choices. Some growers will be able to supply fans three or four years old and already trained to their basic shape. These are ideal for anyone lacking in the confidence to do it themselves, but it really is a lot easier than many gardeners think. Rather than spending huge sums on a ready-trained tree, I would much rather buy a single-stemmed maiden and have the fun of doing it myself. Believe me, the initial training is the easiest part of all.

Feeding

In the early stages, it's a mistake to feed too generously, since this only results in over-vigorous growth. Again, I simplify feeding by using a general fertiliser supplemented by regular mulches of manure or compost. I put on about 2oz. per sq. yd (60gm per sq. m.) of blood, fish and bone fertiliser in March plus a generous helping of manure.

Thinning

In a year when we escape late frosts, plums can bear enormous crops. If the fruits are not thinned, the result can be a vast quantity of small, tasteless fruits and broken branches caused by the weight of the crop. And broken branches mean the risk of silver leaf.

I think that thinning is one of the really essential jobs on plums, but I must confess that I rarely have the courage to do much until after the June drop – which again, generally occurs in July! If I have the time and the inclination, I will remove in June those odd few damaged, misshapen or tiny fruits that are obviously not going to make anything. Generally I happily accept the 'white feather' and pluck up courage to complete the job in July after the natural drop. Thin to leave the fruits about 3in. (7.5cm.) apart. It seems a bit drastic at the time, but they soon fill out to give, certainly as heavy a crop as they would if left unthinned and of much better quality and flavour.

Support

As with apples and pears, support of heavily-laden branches could avert disaster. Without wishing to rub it in too much, the silver leaf problem makes it even more important.

Pruning

To reduce the risk of infection, trees should be pruned at a time when they are growing strongly. Wounds will then callus over quickly and the despicable fungus will be foiled again.

The best time is between April and the end of August.

Dwarf pyramids

As with apples and pears, pyramid plums have a central leader and the side-branches are pruned to leave them longer at the bottom of the tree than the top, rather like a Christmas tree.

Start with a single-stemmed maiden or if the trees have side-branches, choose one with the side-shoots evenly distributed round the tree like the spokes of a wheel.

Late in March after planting, prune the main stem back to about 5ft (1.5m.) and remove right back to the trunk, any side-branches that are less than 1½ft (45cm.) from the ground. The remaining side branches, if any, should be cut back to about half their length.

In August of the same year, shorten the branch leaders to leave about 8in. (20cm.) of the current season's growth and any sub-laterals to 6in. (15cm.). Always cut back to a downward or an outward facing bud.

If there are branches near the top of the tree that have a very narrow angle with the main stem, they can be removed altogether. Narrow angles are weak and could be a source of future breakages.

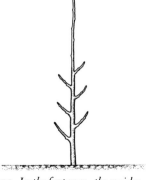

50 *In the first year, the maiden tree is allowed to grow naturally*

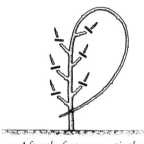

51 *After the first season, tie the main shoot down to form a hoop*

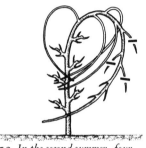

52 *In the second summer, four more shoots are tied down*

53 *In the third spring, the main shoot can be pruned back, cutting the tie at the same time*

The winter pruning of the main stem which was done during the dormant season on apples and pears, is delayed until April with plums, again because it reduces the risk of infection. This is simply a case of cutting it back to leave about a third of last season's growth. This leader pruning is done every April until the tree is as high as you can reach, after which it is cut back quite viciously to about 1in. (2.5cm.) every May to prevent it becoming out of hand.

In the last week in July every year, the branch leaders are again shortened to leave about 8in. (20cm.) of the current season's growth and the sub-laterals to 6in. (15cm.).

An interesting method of pruning trees on the dwarfing stock Pixy was developed by Bonham Bazeley at Highfield Nurseries. He experimented with a method of restricting the flow of sap through the tree to force it into fruiting. This, of course, is the principle employed on cordons which are grown at an angle for that reason.

In the first year the tree is allowed to grow naturally (50). After the first season, the main shoot is bent down into a hoop and tied to the base of the plant (51). This induces plenty of shoots to grow on the top of the curve and fruiting spurs to grow at the base of the main shoot. The spurs are cut back to three buds in April.

In the second summer, while the shoots are still pliable, four are selected and bent down in their turn to form more hoops (52). Any extra shoots are cut back to three buds to form spurs in August.

In the third spring, the main shoot is pruned back, but still retains its curve, looking rather like a walking stick. Again, excess branches can be pruned back to form fruiting spurs (53).

It's an interesting method of producing early fruit and should be particularly useful for growing trees in tubs.

Fans

Before embarking on fan training, bear in mind that they do take a fair bit of time and need constant attention to training and tying in. They are not a proposition for the gardener with little time, but very well worth the extra attention required if you can do it.

Start with a maiden (one-year-old) tree. It should be planted near to, but not right against a fence or wall, and horizontal wires at 9in. (23cm.) intervals fixed to the wall for support.

If the tree has two strong, well-placed branches about 18in. (45cm.) above the ground and opposite each other, they can be used as the first two branches, which make up the main framework of the fan. Cut them back after planting to a downward pointing bud to leave about 1½–2ft (45–60cm.). These are then tied to canes which are in turn tied to the wires at an angle of about 20 degrees to the horizontal to form an open V-shape. The main stem is then cut out just above the two selected branches.

If there are no suitable branches, cut back to a bud about 18in. (45cm.) above the ground (54). During the summer, branches will grow out and two should be retained to form the main framework, while the others are pinched back to two leaves. This is simply a case of removing the growing tips with your fingers when they are still green and soft. Once the two shoots that are to form the main framework are about 18 in. (45cm.) long, the main stem can be cut back to just above them (55).

From now on, pruning is aimed at covering the wall (56). Start by removing all the shoots that are growing straight out away from the wall or straight in towards it. This is done as soon as growth starts in early April. Space the shoots out evenly and tie them in with soft string. You'll have to go back to those ties from time to time to check that they're not restricting growth and that the string is still intact.

Any shoots that are not needed to fill a space can be pinched back when they've made half-a-dozen leaves, just taking out the growing tip with your fingers.

When any shoots outgrow their space, do the same thing, just pinching out the growing tip.

At the end of the season, when the fruit has been picked, cut out any dead wood and shorten those shoots you've pinched back by about half.

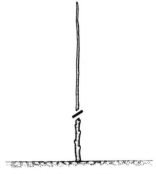

54 *Cut back the maiden tree to about 18in. (45cm.) after planting*

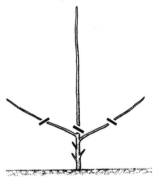

55 *Select two side shoots and train them in. When they are 18in. long, cut back the centre stem. Cut the side branches back to 18in. (45cm.)*

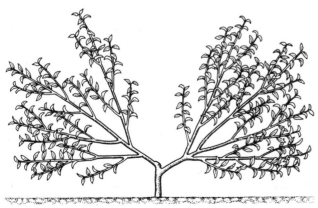

56 *Tie in shoots to cover the wall. Pinch out those growing towards or away from the wall and unwanted shoots to 6 leaves*

Harvesting

Pick fruit destined for the pot or for jam-making, a little before it's fully ripe. Eating fruit is best left until it's fully ripe and eaten straight away. It will not keep for more than a few days once picked.

Pests and diseases

Again, I have suggested a spray programme as the most effective way of dealing with pests and diseases. In order to cut down as much as possible on the number of chemicals used, I have stuck to the two ICI products recommended for apples and pears – Picket and Nimrod 'T'.

There is no need to use the fungicide until late June, but the insecticide should be applied at white bud stage, at petal fall, seven days later, and in late June. The fungicide is added in late June to control plum rust if it is seen. The pests and diseases controlled are listed below together with the symptoms of attack.

Aphids: the insects can be seen clustered on shoot-tips and buds and they cause severe curling of leaves. They generally exude a honeydew which acts as a host for sooty-mould fungus.

Plum fruit moth: often, the first that is seen is the maggot in the fruit, so a preventive spray is essential.

Plum sawfly: leaves large, messy holes in fruit, which mainly drop.

Plum rust: causes small yellow spots on the top surface of leaves, which fall prematurely.

As you expected, there are some pests and diseases not controlled by the spray programme, but these only need treatment if and when they are seen.

Red spider mite: the same mite that attacks apples. If seen, spray with Pirimiphos methyl (ICI Sybol 2).

Silver leaf: causes a silvering of the leaves which may go brown. There is a progressive die-back of branches and when cut, the wood inside is stained brown or purple. Avoid it by pruning during the summer and by avoiding breakages. Paint all wounds with fungicide paint (PBI Arbrex) after pruning. If a tree is attacked, cut back the affected branch to clean wood and paint with Arbrex.

Bacterial canker: causes round, brown spots on leaves which eventually fall away to form 'shot-holes'. The following spring, brown, sunken cankers will appear on branches and they will exude a gummy substance. Later, branches begin to die back. The only treatment is to cut out diseased wood.

Plum Pox: is a virus disease causing yellow spots or rings on leaves. The fruit becomes pock-marked with brown patches under the skin. It generally falls early and tastes bitter. Alas, no cure I'm afraid. It is a notifiable disease so, if you detect signs, contact the local office of the Ministry of Agriculture.

DAMSONS

The sharp, distinctive flavour of damsons make them an ideal fruit for bottling and jam-making. They are grown in exactly the same way as plums.

Varieties

The following are self-fertile.

Merryweather: certainly the most popular of damson varieties but for me, not the best of flavours. A good heavy, regular cropper ready for picking in late August.

King of the Damsons: medium sized, sweet fruits and a good yield, make this a fine garden variety. Crops in mid-September.

APRICOTS

Though perhaps a bit more 'up-market' than plums, apricots are grown in exactly the same way.

Though it may be possible to grow them as free-standing dwarf pyramids in the south of the country, it's perhaps safer to allot them some wall space and grow them as fans.

If plums need good drainage, apricots are ten times fussier. It is essential to grow them on freely-drained soil prepared by digging a good deep trench at the foot of the wall and filling the bottom with drainage material such as broken brick or pebbles. They are notorious for suffering from die-back of the branches and this is much more apparent on badly-drained soil.

Varieties

All varieties are self-fertile but, since they flower early, there may not be too many pollinating insects about. It's worth doing the job yourself by transferring pollen from one flower to another with a paint-brush. Protect the flowers from frost by covering with a fine net – old net curtains are ideal.

Farmingdale: fruits early and has a delicious flavour. It is perhaps less susceptible to die-back than other varieties.

Moor Park: the most popular and freely available variety. Large juicy fruits of excellent flavour, but alas, somewhat susceptible to die-back.

8 CHERRIES

If you're blessed with a very large garden, a sweet cherry tree is definitely for you. If, like most of us, your plot is small, forget it. If you have a large, south or west-facing wall, you could grow a fan-shaped tree, but even then, you'll need anything from 18–25ft (5.5–7.5m.)

Bush or half-standard sweet-cherries make big trees, but if you have room – and you'll need at least 15ft (4.5m.) all round it and possibly more – it is one of the most attractive of fruit trees. The deep red bark makes it a fine feature in winter, in the spring it will be loaded with superb blossom, in the summer there is the attraction of the cherries themselves while the autumn brings rich leaf colouring.

Unfortunately, there is one other big problem apart from size. The fruits are much sought-after by birds. Once the word gets around the avian underworld that there are ripe cherries going begging, they'll come in their droves to make quite sure you harvest not a single fruit. Netting even a fan trained tree is a problem because of their size, and a bush or half-standard is out of the question.

Having tried assiduously to put you off, I must add that the picking season is fairly short so, if you take steps to scare birds off, you may well get away with it and harvest most of the crop before they become used to your deterrents. I have tried strips of polythene hung in the trees where they'll flap in the wind and this seems to work quite well for the few days it's necessary.

Tree shapes

I'm sure that the most practical and productive method of growing sweet cherries is as a fan. This way you are in some control of the size of the tree and it is an easier job to protect the fruits from birds.

If you have the space and want to grow a cherry for decorative as well as productive purposes, perhaps in the lawn, it's best to grow them in pyramid shape (notice that I avoid the misleading term '*dwarf* pyramid') with the minimum of pruning. Just like plums, cherries are also very prone to attack from silver leaf disease, and the minimum of pruning will help prevent entry of the fungus and, at the same time tend to keep the trees from growing too vigorously. Remember, the harder you prune in winter, the more growth the tree will make.

Varieties

For the small garden, the choice of varieties is not wide. The problem is one of pollination. Small gardens are hardly suitable for one tree and the very thought of two sweet cherries in a modern, postage-stamp plot is laughable. So, there are just two alternatives. The first, and in my view, by far the most sensible, is to grow the only self-fertile variety – Stella. Alternatively, the much smaller acid cherry, Morello will pollinate sweet cherries, but it flowers too late for most. Since cherries are also subject to virus diseases, it's also important to choose varieties that come within the EMLA scheme for ensuring virus-free stock. Make sure the trees you buy have the EMLA label. So, the list is cut down to just a couple of varieties.

Stella: fruits in late July, bearing black fruits of a good size but perhaps not the best flavour of them all. It's a vigorous grower, but being self-fertile, it does at least dispense with the necessity of growing two trees.

Bigarreau Gaucher: produces large, black cherries which are juicy and very well flavoured. It flowers late, so could be valuable where frost is a problem. It crops in July and is pollinated by Morello.

Rootstocks

Much has been written about the new 'dwarfing' rootstock Colt. Be warned. Though it certainly does have some effect on the limitation of vigour, it does *not* produce dwarf trees. In fact, they will be something like 15–20ft (4.5–6.5m.) tall and 12–15ft (3.5–4.5m.) wide, depending on the variety that's budded onto the stock. However, with cherries, small is most definitely beautiful and this stock is a couple of steps nearer what we want. It also crops earlier in its life and seems to produce branches which have a wider and therefore stronger angle with the trunk.

I suspect that, until something even better comes along, few nurseries will be offering cherries budded onto anything else but Colt for sale to gardeners.

Planting

Sweet cherries are deep-rooting plants so they need a deep, fertile soil. They require lots of moisture so heavy soils will be more successful than light, sandy ones.

Ideally, they need a warm, sunny spot, so if you live in a cold area, stick to a fan shape and plant it against a south or west-facing wall.

Feeding

Because of their vigorous growth, cherries should never be overfed, especially with nitrogen, the growth-promoting element. I feed with my old faithful blood, fish and bone in February and I restrict it to 2oz. per sq. yd (60gm per sq. m.)

Again, mulch annually with manure or compost to add the trace elements and to help retain water.

It has always been thought that cherries must have a limey soil for best results. In fact, though some lime is acceptable, too much can lead to magnesium deficiency. This shows up as a yellowing of the leaf tissue between the veins. If this occurs, spray with a foliar feed like PBI Fillip.

Watering is important in the early summer and especially so with trees grown against a wall. Here they often tend to dry out because of the extra warmth and the fact that rain doesn't reach the roots too easily. It may well be necessary to water by hand, but you should stop once the fruit starts to swell, or it may split. Bear in mind too, that if water is applied by hand, it's important to really soak the soil to get it right down to the root zone.

Pruning

Because of the risk of infection by silver leaf disease and of bacterial canker, the less pruning that is done, the better. Bush trees are best allowed to grow with a central stem like a dwarf-pyramid apple. Leave the trees entirely unpruned for the first few years and later, only when it becomes necessary, remove crowded, crossing, dead or diseased branches.

If pruning is needed to keep the tree within bounds, do it in July.

Pruning of fan-trained sweet cherries is exactly as described for plums in Chapter 7.

Harvesting

Allow cherries to stay on the tree as long as possible to give them the chance to develop their full flavour, but make sure you catch them before they split.

They will not store and deteriorate fairly rapidly, so they should be eaten straight away. And that's no hardship at all!

Pests and diseases

Fortunately, there are few pests and diseases to worry about and a regular spray programme is unnecessary.

Blackfly: in my experience, once attacked by blackfly one year, they can be expected every year. So, spray them as soon as you see the first attack and the next year spray at the white bud stage whether they are there or not. ICI Sybol 2 or Picket will see them off. Normally you'll easily see the insects clustered in their hundreds round the shoot-tips and under the leaves which curl quite severely.

Winter moth: as with apples, the grubs burrow into the blossoms and tend to spin leaves together. They can be controlled in the same way with Picket.

Bacterial canker: the same progressive die-back and gummy extrusions as in plums. Cut out and burn infected wood and, if the disease is troublesome, spray at leaf fall and during August, September and October with Bordeaux Mixture or copper fungicide.

Silver leaf: symptoms and control as for plums.

ACID CHERRIES
Growing cooking cherries has few of the problems for gardeners that are presented by their sweeter cousins. The trees are much smaller, less demanding and self-fertile. They make attractive trees and the fruit is absolutely delicious when cooked or bottled. They have the added advantage that they can be grown against a north-facing wall where not much else will do.

Tree shapes
Though there is no reason why trees should not be grown in bush form, they are generally grown as fans. For my money, this is certainly the best bet, since it's absolutely essential to net them against birds. In the first years of growing them, I was a little lax about the netting with the result that my carefully nurtured crop disappeared overnight. Fans will only grow about 10ft (3m.) tall, so they are no problem to net.

Varieties
Morello: this is really the only variety on offer generally these days. It is certainly the best of the cooking types cropping in late July or August, reliably and heavily. As I have already mentioned, it is self-fertile, so there is no need for more than one tree.

Rootstocks
Morello cherries are also compatible with the new Colt rootstock and this is certainly the most favourable for garden planting.

Planting

Though acid cherries will do well in just about any situation, the fact that they will thrive on a north-facing wall means that is generally where they finish up. It's too good a quality to waste.

They are not nearly so fussy about soil as the sweet cherries either, though proper preparation as described in Chapter 2 will be well repaid.

Feeding

They have a slightly higher demand for nitrogen than sweet cherries, so put on 3oz. per sq. yd (90gm per sq. m.) of blood, fish and bone in February and supplement it with an annual mulch of manure or compost.

Pruning

Acid cherries differ from sweet varieties in that they fruit on wood made the year previously. They should therefore be pruned like fan-trained peaches. The only difference is that the side-shoots can be left a little closer at about 2in. (5cm.) apart. (See Chapter 9).

Pests and diseases

Acid cherries suffer the same ills as sweet varieties and should be treated in the same way.

9 PEACHES

According to the Oxford English Dictionary, the word 'peach' means, in colloquial terms, 'a person or thing of superlative quality'. A fitting accolade for this most exotic of our fruits.

The supreme quality of the fruit gives the impression that this is a delicate plant requiring all the pampering you would give to a new-born babe. In fact, the tree itself is as hardy as old boots. The only problem arises from the fact that it flowers very early, round about March or April, so the flowers are very subject to frost damage.

Tree shapes

Because of the high risk of frost damage and the resulting loss of crop, there is really only one satisfactory way of growing peaches. They need a south-facing wall to give the flowers all the protection of reflected and stored heat, so the best bet is to grow them as a fan.

In the deep south or the West country, it may be possible to get away with a free-standing bush tree, but even then there is still the risk of losing the whole crop every so often.

Nectarines, which are really only clean-shaven peaches, need exactly the same sort of protection and indeed, they are grown in a similar way. The only difference is that, because they are slightly smaller fruited, the trees can be allowed to bear more fruits.

It is possible to buy fan-trained peaches and nectarines already started, but you'll have to search them out. Alas, the noble art of pruning and training is fast disappearing, so you may have to resort to buying a bush tree or preferably a one-year-old, and training it yourself.

Varieties

Peaches and nectarines are self-fertile, setting fruit on their own pollen, so there is no need to grow two trees.

Because they were so popular with Victorian gardeners, there are dozens of old varieties that sound delicious. But try finding them! Many, of course, were grown under glass in those days, when they could be afforded the luxury of a little heat at flowering time and have now gone out of fashion in favour of slightly hardier, heavier cropping varieties. Nurserymen's lists may be shorter these days, but you can be sure of better fruiting outdoors.

Duke of York: one of the earliest to fruit and relatively hardy, this variety is suitable for growing outside or in a cold greenhouse. The fruits are large and deep crimson with yellow flesh. Flavour and texture are excellent.

Peregrine: fruits slightly later than Duke of York and is often recommended as one of the easiest to grow outside. However, don't be misled into thinking that it will escape frost damage. Fruits are large, deep red with greenish-white flesh. Very juicy with a fine flavour.

Rochester: probably one of the hardiest of peaches and flowering a little later than most, but still susceptible to damage. Generally considered the easiest to grow but perhaps not of equal quality. The fruit is yellow with a deep crimson flush and the flavour is fair.

Early Rivers: cropping in late July, this is probably the best of nectarines. The greenish-yellow fruit flushes deep red and the flesh is juicy and well flavoured. Can be grown outside or under glass.

Lord Napier: not quite as hardy as the others and therefore best grown under glass or on a sunny wall in the southern counties. The fruit is large and the flavour undoubtedly the best of all.

Rootstocks
Peaches are grown on the same rootstocks as plums but, being less vigorous there are none of the problems of excess growth, even on the more vigorous stocks.

St Julien A: a semi-dwarfing stock which induces the tree to crop slightly earlier in its life.

Brompton: the most vigorous rootstock. Ideal if you have a large wall to cover.

Pixy: some nurserymen now offer peaches and nectarines on the new dwarfing stock. It will produce quite small trees which come into fruiting much earlier. Ideal where space is limited or for bush trees in the south, but perhaps too small for normal fan-training.

Planting
Good drainage is essential for success with peaches, so it's worthwhile taking a bit of trouble over preparing the site.

In new houses, it is particularly important. You will often find that the builders, when they dig the footings for the house, simply refill the trenches with subsoil, so you could be planting in heavy, sticky clay. If their feet are wet and cold, peaches will simply sit and sulk. They'll grow little and they'll never provide you with a decent crop. Show them you care and you'll have a friend for life.

The best way is to dig a trench about 2–3ft (60–90cm.) wide, 10–15ft (3–4.5m.) long and a good spade deep. Break up the bottom and lighten the soil if necessary with coarse grit. On top of this, spread a good layer of well-rotted manure or compost before replacing the soil. If the soil to be replaced is heavy, mix in a bit of peat or some more manure or compost. It really is worthwhile getting them off to a flying start.

Plant about 9in. (23cm.) away from the wall to give the roots a chance to get water early on. Later, they'll push their roots out well clear of the dry wall-bottom, but in the first couple of years, you must be prepared to water by hand if the soil gets really dry.

Wires must be fixed to the wall to facilitate training and these should be at about 9in. (23cm.) intervals. Use strong galvanised wire and fix it either to wooden battens plugged to the wall, or with vine-eyes.

Feeding

As with all fruit trees, it's necessary to try to get a balance between good growth each year and a heavy crop. If the trees are overfed, they tend to make a lot of growth at the expense of fruit while lack of food means that growth is slow and there will not be enough branches to bear a good crop. What I do is to try to get rapid growth early on and then reduce the feeding to encourage fruiting. In the early stages, I feed with blood, fish and bone in February at 4oz. per sq.yd (120gm per sq.m.). I also mulch generously with manure or compost each year to add the necessary trace elements and to help retain water.

After a couple of years, when the tree is beginning to get well furnished, the annual feed can be reduced by half.

Adequate supplies of water are essential and, as I have already suggested, it may be necessary to water by hand, especially in the early stages.

Thinning

In a good year, when frosts are few, peaches can produce masses of fruit. If they are all left on the tree, the size will be drastically reduced and they will lack flavour and juiciness. You must steel yourself to remove a few.

Ideally, you need about one fruit every 9in. (23cm.). The thinning is done in two stages, first when the fruits are about the size of a cob-nut and later when they have swelled to walnut size. There may be some dropping so it's unwise to do it all at once. If you can't bring yourself to take them off at the first stage, make sure you don't miss them at the second.

Start by removing fruits that will not, because of their position, make satisfactory peaches. Those, for example, that are placed right between a branch and the wall will never have the space to swell. Then reduce clusters of fruit to singles, leaving overall, about twice as many fruits as will eventually be needed. Later on, when they begin to swell and a few have dropped naturally, it will be quite safe to complete the job. As with apples, the weight of the thinned fruit will be equal to an unthinned crop and the quality a thousand times better.

Frost protection
The danger time with fruit is when it's in flower. During March and early April frost is more or less inevitable, so it's worth protecting the flowers every night. A couple of layers of fine-mesh netting is often adequate, but a sheet of hessian or even an old bed-sheet is safer. If it's fixed to a couple of long poles it can be unrolled each night and the poles leaned against the wall. Don't forget to roll it up again early in the morning.

Pollination
Though peaches and nectarines are both capable of setting fruit with their own pollen, the weather is often too cold at flowering time to tempt pollinating insects out to do their work.

Though you'll get some natural pollination, it's best to make sure and do it by hand. It's a laborious job to be sure, but quite enjoyable on a warm Sunday morning and much more productive than washing the car! Simply go round each flower with a soft paintbrush, gently brushing the centres of each to transfer some pollen. If the weather is particularly dry, which can sometimes happen at that time of year believe it or not, a spray over the flowers with clear water afterwards helps to make the pollen viable.

Pruning
Instructions for pruning peaches are always totally incomprehensible. You'll no doubt have to read this bit eight times before you begin to grasp it, but I'll do my best. It's a job that requires care and regular attention but, once you get the hang of it, is much, much easier than it sounds. Don't ever be put off growing peaches or nectarines because this part of the job sounds difficult. Once you start doing it, it all comes crystal clear.

It helps greatly to know the principles behind pruning.

There are two stages in the pruning programme. In the first years, the emphasis is on making a framework to cover the wall. There is no need to worry about pruning for fruit in this time, and if any are formed, they are probably best removed.

Pruning back to a bud will stimulate that bud into growth and the harder you cut back, the stronger growth will be. It's essential to be able to differentiate between a fruit bud and a wood bud. Fruit buds are fatter and rounder and will not grow out at all. Wood buds are pointed and narrow and will produce a new shoot.

After the framework has been built up, the tree is pruned to produce fruit. The reason for this regular pruning at the fruiting stage is that peaches bear their fruit on wood made the previous year. The object then, is to cut out the wood that has fruited, training one-year-old wood in its place and encouraging the production of new wood for fruiting the following year.

To make the framework, start by buying a one-year-old tree. If it has two conveniently placed, strong branches about 18in. (45cm.) above the ground, and growing opposite each other, they can be used as the first main branches. If not, cut back to a strong bud about 18in. (45cm.) above the ground (57). In the following year, two branches will grow out to form those first two arms. This obviously takes an extra year so it's better if possible to buy a tree which already has those two strategically placed branches.

So, whether it's immediately after planting or a year later, we now have a tree with two branches coming out one either side of the trunk. Cut these back to about 18in. (45cm.) to a downward-pointing bud and tie them in (58). They are, like the

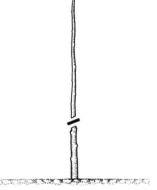

57 *Cut back maiden trees to 18in. (45cm.) after planting, leaving three good buds*

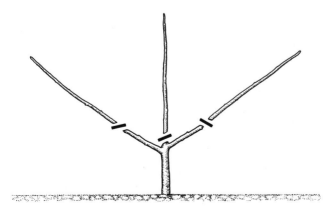

58 *Tie in the two 'arms' to 45 degrees and cut back in winter to 18in. (45cm.). Cut out the centre completely*

71

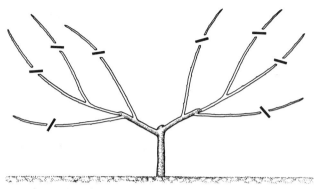

59 *Select six branches about 1ft (30cm.) apart and tie them in. Prune them back in winter to 18in. (45cm.)*

plum described in Chapter 7, tied to canes which are, in turn tied to the wires at an angle of something like 20 degrees above the horizontal. The rest of the tree which will be growing straight upwards, is pruned right out and the wound painted with PBI Arbrex.

First summer: from each of those two branches that are left, you're looking for four new shoots. First of all, a good strong shoot should grow out of the end. After it has grown about 4in. (10cm.), start tying it to the cane to continue the 'arm'. Then, you want two shoots growing upwards from each arm. The first should be something like 1ft (30cm.) from the middle of the fan, and the second about 1ft (30cm.) on from that. Tie those into new canes tied to the wires and you can begin to see the shape of a fan (59).

In between those two shoots but facing downwards, select another shoot and tie in the same way. Other shoots are not needed and should be rubbed out while they are still soft.

First winter: cut back the framework branches you have tied in, leaving them about 18in. (45cm.) long.

Second summer: continue to tie in the extensions to those eight main framework branches. On either side of each branch, select side-shoots so that they are placed no more than 4in. (10cm.) apart and tie them in. Anything else should be rubbed out while it is still green and soft (60). Also rub out any shoots that are growing directly away from the wall or directly towards it. This is a strictly two-dimensional tree.

Second winter: new growth from the main framework branches is again cut back to leave about half the wood that was made last year. From now on, we prune for fruit.

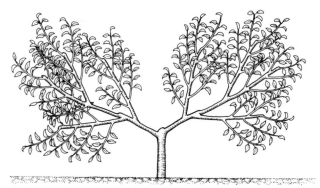

60 *Select side-shoots about 4in. (10cm.) apart and tie them in. Rub out other shoots. In winter, prune all new growth by about half*

61 *On established trees, those side-shoots you have selected and tied in 4in. (10cm.) apart are allowed to grow four to six leaves and are then pinched back. A shoot growing near the base is tied in as a replacement*

Third summer: those side-shoots that have been tied in 4in. (10cm.) apart are the fruit-bearers. When they've made about four to six leaves and have a shoot coming out from the base, they can be pinched back by just nipping out the growing point. The fruit will be borne on the nipped shoot while the new shoot growing from its base will be tied in to replace it next year (61). After fruiting, the wood that has borne the fruit is cut right out just above the new shoot and this takes its turn to become next year's fruit-bearer.

Established plants: from now on, this pattern is repeated. The aim is to replace the shoot that is fruiting this year with another growing from its base. In summer these new shoots are tied in, while the wood that is to fruit is pinched back to four to six leaves. In winter, the wood that has fruited is cut right out (62).

When the main framework arms reach the end of the wall, they too are treated like side-shoots, pinching back in the summer to four to six leaves.

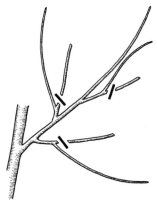

62 *In winter, cut out the shoots that have fruited and tie in the replacements*

Harvesting

You have to be vigilant at harvest time. Being soft, peaches bruise badly if allowed to fall, so as they get near picking time, have a look every day. Test for readiness in much the same way as apples but a lot more gently. Just cup the fruit in the palm of your hand and lift it. When it's ripe it will come away easily.

If you keep them in a cool spot, they'll keep in good condition for a few days, but not a lot more. They can be frozen in syrup though I must say that I've never managed to keep mine long enough to try!

Pests and diseases

There are really only two problems with peaches most years and they can be controlled with our 'cocktail' of ICI Picket and Nimrod 'T'. Though it isn't really necessary to spray against aphids until they become a problem, I mix the insecticide with the fungicide as a preventive measure and am rarely troubled. It is certainly necessary to spray regularly against Peach Leaf Curl, especially if it has occurred before.

Spray as soon as the buds open and at two-week intervals until leaf-fall.

Aphids: insects are seen underneath the leaves which tend to curl.

Peach leaf curl: a more common disease since the Clean Air Act removed the sulphur from the atmopshere. It shows as bright red blisters on the leaves, which curl and eventually fall. The time to spray against it is *before* you see it. You can almost guarantee it will find your plants eventually.

Red spider mite: in a dry year, these tiny mites can be a problem. They are very hard to see individually but they mass together to form a reddish haze. The leaves become mottled with yellow and eventually fall. They don't like wet weather, so they can be discouraged by spraying the plants with water, but if you see an infestation, be on the safe side and spray immediately with Sybol 2.

10 STRAWBERRIES

If you have a brand new garden and can't wait to pick your first fruit, make a start with strawberries. Plant them in August and you'll be picking your first fruits in June the following year. With a little gentle persuasion, you can even get them a month or so earlier than that.

And, apart from their enthusiasm for work, they are also the most versatile of fruits. They can be grown in tiny spaces on the patio or balcony, even on the windowsill. Simple and cheap to grow, there is no reason why even the tiniest garden should not have its strawberry patch.

Varieties
Strawberries are also included in the Ministry of Agriculture scheme for ensuring healthy, virus-free stock. They are very subject to virus diseases, so it's important to buy from a specialist grower who submits his plants for certification.

Actually, the Certification Scheme includes only field-grown runners and these are lifted from September onwards. If you want fruit the following year, it's important to plant in August, so you won't be able to buy certified plants at that time. But, if you buy from a grower who intends to submit his plants for certification, you can be very sure that he will have regularly sprayed his plants against aphids – the virus carrier – and that they will be clean.

Above all, never, never accept runners from a friend, and be wary of propagating too long from your own plants. There's no cure for virus diseases, so they must be avoided at all costs.

There are dozens of varieties to choose from and I can't claim to have grown them all. However, I grow about six new varieties every year and I've selected the half-a-dozen that have done best for me over the years. The six varieties grown together will give as long a period of harvesting as is possible, especially if the earliest are forced in a greenhouse and later under cloches. Varieties are listed in order of ripening.

Pantagruella: not the heaviest cropping variety, but worth its place because of its very early harvesting period. The plants are sometimes labelled by the nurseryman as 'compact' which, in plain language means small. If possible, buy the largest runners you can, and they'll give you a very good crop of well-flavoured fruits. An excellent variety for forcing.

Tamella: produces very high yields of excellent flavour. The fruits are quite large, especially if they are watered well. It has one problem which I must say I have never encountered in three seasons of growing it. It is said to be subject to attack by a fungus disease that destroys the crown of the plant. If this does occur, I'm afraid that the best method of control is to grow something less susceptible.

Hapil: following on from Tamella, this new variety consistently produces high yields of large, firm, well-flavoured fruits.

Saladin: another consistent and heavy cropper. The fruits are large and well flavoured. They do tend to be somewhat misshapen, which may worry the showman, but this is not really a problem for the gardener growing for the table. It has a high resistance to the virus disease Red Core.

Troubador: not an outstanding cropper though certainly quite acceptable. Its great value lies in its very late cropping time. Flavour is very good and it has shown resistance to virus diseases.

Aromel: though classed as an autumn-fruiting variety, I find that it crops both early in the summer and in the autumn. However, I feel that it's well worth removing the early flowers to increase the size of the later crop. There are other varieties that can be used to pick in summer. Fruits are medium sized and, in my opinion, superb in flavour.

Apart from this half-dozen, I include three other varieties that are quite different for one reason or another.

Totem: the first of a new range of strawberries that can be frozen. If you've ever tried freezing strawberries, you'll know that they come out of the freezer as a soggy mess fit only for purée or giving to the dog if he'll eat it. Totem is quite different. If frozen in a sugar syrup, it remains firm and can be eaten just as it is. Treated in this way it's delicious, though fresh from the plant it possesses a check-shrinking acidity.

Sweetheart: the first normal-sized variety that can be raised from seed to fruit the same season. Seed is sown during January in a heated greenhouse or even on the kitchen windowsill. Planted out in early June, it will produce good crops of well-flavoured fruits the same year.

Alexandria: this is an Alpine strawberry grown in the same way as Sweethheart. The fruits are very small but extremely prolific and they have a quite distinct flavour which I find very good indeed. In a mild autumn/early winter, I have been picking fruits for eating fresh in November.

Planting

I have tried several different methods of growing strawberries at Barnsdale, many of them used successfully by commercial growers. Generally though, they are after a different end product and have different priorities. What we require, is the biggest harvest per square yard of the best quality strawberries, and considerations like labour costs and uniformity of size don't really come into it. So I have come to the conclusion that there is only one way to grow them and that's more or less the traditional way.

I have had my best crops and highest quality fruit from plants set in rows 2ft (60cm.) apart with 18in. (45cm.) between the plants (63). I keep the pathways free of runners which, if left will spread to cover the whole area, resulting in perhaps a bigger total weight of fruit but with individual fruits smaller and of lower quality.

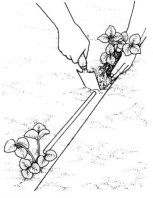

63 *Plant with a trowel setting the plants 2ft (60cm.) apart with 18in. (45cm.) between rows*

Since the plants will be occupying the space for about five or six years, it's worth spending some time preparing it. First of all, make sure that you have got rid of all the perennial weeds. Once something like couch-grass or bellbine gets in the bed, it's the devil's own job to get rid of it. There are now weed-killers that will sort out some of the worst perennial weeds, but it's a lot easier to clean the ground thoroughly before you plant.

The best and surest way to get rid of perennials is to spray them out with something like Murphy Tumbleweed. If it's only annual weeds that are a problem, they are better simply dug in when the ground is prepared.

Though it's a mistake to overfeed strawberries, they do like plenty of moisture, and they insist on good drainage. So, the double-digging technique, working in rotted manure or compost is again the order of the day. If the ground is heavy and lies wet, it pays to make 4ft (1.2m.) wide beds and to raise them above the level of the surrounding soil with the manure and by scraping soil from the paths onto the bed. Just before planting, scatter a dressing of bonemeal at about 3oz. per sq. yd (90gm per sq. m.) and rake it in.

It's important for the soil to be firm and level before planting, so try to allow a few weeks at least for it to settle. If this is impossible, wait until it's reasonably dry – generally not too difficult at strawberry planting time – and tread over it systematically with your weight on your heels, to firm it thoroughly. Then rake it level and you're ready to plant.

The best time for planting is late July or early August and I would certainly not want to delay it much later than the first week in September. If you do, the plants will give a poor crop

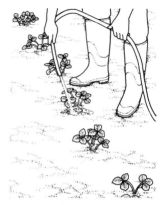

64 *Make sure that the crown of the plant is exactly at soil level and firm the soil around the roots*

65 *After planting water thoroughly to settle the soil round the roots and to ensure adequate moisture*

the following year. In this case, it's really better to remove the flowers that form in that first spring to allow the plants to build up for a good crop the year after.

If you buy plants in August, it's more than likely that they will be pot-grown. When they arrive, unpack them immediately and, if they appear dry, soak them thoroughly. Many plants for August planting come in pots made of compressed peat, and it is vital that they should not be dry at planting time. If they are, they'll be very difficult to wet again once they're in the soil and the roots may well find it difficult to grow out of them.

Plant against a tight line and with a trowel, making sure that the crown of the plant – where the leaves join the roots – is exactly at ground level (64). Too shallow and the roots will be exposed, so establishment will be slow, too low, and wet conditions may well rot the centre of the plant.

It's quite likely at that time of year, that you could experience a spell of dry weather. You could avoid this by timing your holiday for just after planting, when it's bound to pour with rain. A safer way is to put the lawn sprinkler on the plants for an hour or so to water them in thoroughly. Adequate water is essential in those early stages, so you may well have to repeat the dose a few times before the autumn rains come (65).

After planting, I like to mulch the rows with a bit more compost or manure, to conserve moisture and repress weeds.

Feeding

Strawberries don't want a lot of feeding. With too much nitrogen, they will make fine, large plants with masses of leaves.

But, like many other flowering and fruiting plants, if they are growing that well, they see no need to produce new plants from seed. So they take it easy and refuse to expend their energy on flowering and fruiting. Again, what is needed is a balance between a fair-sized plant and a lot of fruit.

Since they have a very efficient and wide-spreading root system, they will more or less forage for their food, so generally an annual dressing of well-rotted manure or compost is all that's needed. They do, however, have a need for potash. That's the element that encourages flowering and fruiting and they'll gobble it up like it's going out of fashion.

So, in this case, I think it's worth investing in a pack of sulphate of potash instead of the faithful blood, fish and bone. It should be applied at about ½oz. per sq. yd (15gm per sq. m.) after the crop has been picked.

The only time it is necessary to use a general fertiliser is if the plants are simply not growing. Frankly, your soil would need to be very poor indeed to warrant it, and I think that I would be inclined to suspect virus disease first as a more likely cause of really poor growth.

Cultivations
It really is essential to keep strawberries free from weeds. They don't like competition and a good, healthy growth of weeds will also prevent air circulation round the plants and this could quickly lead to an attack from fungus diseases.

Annual weeds are easy to control now, so I'm afraid there's no excuse for a dirty strawberry patch. I use a chemical weed-killer called Propachlor (Murphy Covershield) which is applied as granules. Simply scatter them between the plants according to the instructions on the packet, and they'll prevent annual weeds from germinating. Perennial weeds are more difficult and here, I must urge you again to start clean.

Once the plants have started fruiting, the weight of the swelling berries will start to pull the trusses down towards the ground. Here they become prey to the attentions of slugs, they become splashed with soil in wet weather and, worst of all, they are subject to attack from fungus diseases. They should be kept off the ground by mulching round the plants with straw or with a strip of black polythene pushed up round them (66). It's also possible to buy special strawberry mats made from strong tarred paper, which can be slid round the base of the plant. I like straw, because it keeps the fruit well off the ground without impeding the flow of air and at the end of the season it makes a good compost-bin filler and eventually is recycled back into the soil.

66 *Keep the fruits off the ground by mulching with straw or with special strawberry mats*

It's important though, not to mulch round the plants too soon. When they're flowering, there is always the risk of a late frost damaging the flowers. The soil acts like a storage heater, absorbing heat from the sun during the day and slowly releasing it at night.

It could well raise the temperature round the flowers by a degree or so, which is often, at that time of year, enough to prevent damage. A mulch between the plants and nature's central heating system, will deflect the heat and could spell disaster.

Bird protection is one hundred per cent essential. As soon as the fruits start to swell and well before the first ones start to change colour, the whole bed *must* be netted. Plastic strawberry netting will last several years if treated well and it will make the difference between a good harvest and literally nothing at all. I simply weight it down with stones, though I must admit that this doesn't prevent the odd wily squirrel creeping in underneath. Frankly, they take very little and they're such attractive little devils that I grin and bear it.

Pick over the fruits regularly, taking the stalk and calyx (the little 'spider' on the end of the fruit) with it. If you pull off the fruit and leave the 'plug' from the centre, it is likely to attract fungus disease which will soon spread to the remaining fruits.

After picking is over, the beds should be cleaned up thoroughly. Start by removing all the mulching material and then cut the leaves down, to leave just the crown of the plant (67). This may seem a bit drastic, but it's amazing how quickly they regenerate.

Before they stop growing for the winter, they'll have made a strong new growth of leaves. Cut them back with shears or, to save a bit of time, I use a rotary grass cutter set to its highest setting, and then I rake up the leaves and put them on the compost heap.

67 *At the end of the season, cut off the leaves to an inch or so above the crown. A rotary grass cutter does the job quickly*

Forcing

When strawberries are plentiful in the garden, the prices in the shops tend to plummet. But, early in the season, you'll need to take out a second mortgage to afford a punnet or two. However, there's no reason at all why you shouldn't beat the commercial boys at their own game and grow your own early crop.

The very earliest come from the heated greenhouse, though it is possible to grow them on the kitchen windowsill. If you do, don't expect such good crops because the light levels will be much lower than in the greenhouse.

Plants should be potted in late July or early August. I put

them into 7in. (18cm.) pots of Levington compost, or if I have a growing bag that has housed an early crop of tomatoes, I re-use that, planting three plants per bag.

The plants must stay outside the house until the middle of February. Strawberries need a cold period before they will initiate flower buds, so don't be in too much of a hurry to get them going. The only danger during the winter is excess wet which can rot the crowns of the plants. To avoid it, I simply lay the pots on their sides to keep them dry, or rig up an open-ended cloche over the top of growing bags. Of course, they shouldn't be allowed to become bone-dry, so keep an eye on them and give them a drink if they need it.

They should need no feeding until the fruits start to swell and then I give them a weak feed of high potash tomato ferti-liser.

When they're in flower, they will need pollinating. This is generally not a problem in the greenhouse, since there are usually enough insects around to do it for you, but on the kitchen windowsill, it's safest to transfer pollen from flower to flower with a soft paint brush.

Don't expect an enormous crop from them. It'll be nothing like as heavy as the outside crop, but worth about three times as much compared to shop prices. After fruiting, the plants will be exhausted, so they are best discarded.

After the forced crop, the next earliest will be those grown under cloches. Plant them out at much the same distances as the outside crop, though this will depend largely on the dimensions of the cloches. Bear in mind that, if the rows need to be a bit closer, the plants in the rows can be spread out a little, or vice versa.

I use polythene tunnel cloches which are just about the cheapest cover possible. You can easily make your own with a few lengths of 12 gauge wire and a polythene cloche cover obtainable at any garden centre.

Again, don't cover the plants until February. They should then be cloched, not forgetting to close the ends of the rows. As soon as the plants start to flower, it will be necessary to ventilate on sunny days. This serves not only to lower the temperature, but to allow pollinating insects to get in to do their job.

All other cultivations are exactly as for plants grown outside.

If you have chosen an autumn-fruiting variety to extend the picking season, you may well find that your cloches will come in useful to extend the season at the other end of the year to prevent frost and wet from damaging the ripening fruit.

A new development

One of the interesting new developments tried at Barnsdale recently involved growing frozen strawberries. Nothing to do with fruits grown for the freezer, it is a technique used by some commercial growers to time exactly the picking date of the fruit.

What happens is this. The plants are grown normally and lifted in winter. They are then deep frozen for a period, thawed out and planted again. The process is repeated except that, after coming out of the freezer the second time, they are sold for planting. The amazing thing is that they will then fruit exactly eight weeks after planting.

I planted in mid-August and, sure enough, I was picking ripe strawberries in mid-October. The plants then revert in the second season to normal ripening times. They are a little more expensive than ordinary plants and you'll need to search them out from a specialist grower, but an ideal way of extending the season or of ensuring that you have home-grown fruit for that big occasion.

Growing in containers

The strawberry barrel has been around a long time, and is the ideal way of growing your own in restricted spaces or even if you have no garden at all. They make a very decorative feature on the patio or balcony enabling you to grow dozens of plants in a space no bigger than the container.

An old wooden beer barrel with holes cut in the sides is ideal, but these days hard to find. There are several plastic alternatives that are easier to obtain and do exactly the same job.

When filling them, make the compost very open. I like to mix a fair amount of strawy manure in with John Innes No. 2 potting compost, to ensure a free root run and to enable the water to get right down to the bottom.

Plant through the holes in August and grow them in much the same way as those grown in the open ground. You'll have to ensure that the barrel gets watered regularly and it's a good idea to give them a liquid feed of tomato fertiliser a couple of times during the season.

Propagation

If you're going to propagate your own plants, in my view, it's only worth doing it once from each set of bought-in plants and even then, you're chancing your arm. The problem is the constant one of virus disease. These incurable ailments are carried by greenfly and will devastate your crop. Since there is no cure, the plants can only be thrown away. To make matters worse, some viruses are carried in the soil by eelworms so, if you plant even guaranteed clean stock in the same piece of land, you run the risk of re-infection. It's all very well advising that new plants should be planted as far away from the infected soil as possible, but most of us don't have that amount of room. The best bet, then is to take very great care that the infection never occurs in the first place.

Frankly, the only time I ever propagate from my existing plants is when I need a few plants for forcing in pots. Other than that, I play safe and buy in guaranteed new plants.

For this purpose, because I want to lift and replant in July or August, I propagate straight into small pots. If it's later, bare-rooted plants you want, there will be plenty of self-rooted runners to choose from.

All you need do, is to fill a pot with either soil-less compost or preferably John Innes No.2, and sink it to ground level next to the mother plant. Then select a good runner and peg it into the compost with a bent-wire staple (68). Cut back the remaining runner which would otherwise grow on to produce more, and remove the other runners from the mother plant. Make sure the pot is not allowed to dry out, and when it has rooted, sever it from the mother plant.

68 *To propagate into pots, simply peg a runner into the compost-filled pot, using a wire staple*

Pests and diseases

With strawberries, I again think it's worth spraying as a preventive measure rather than waiting for an attack. Aphids carry virus diseases, so by the time you see them, they may have done their dirty work of transmitting the disease. Botrytis or Grey Mould, is a fungus disease that attacks fruits and stems. Once it is seen on the fruits, it's too late to spray, so it is well worthwhile coating the plants with fungicide beforehand, as a preventive measure.

Since ICI's Nimrod 'T' is not recommended for controlling botrytis, and it is not a good idea to mix products from two different manufacturers, I'm afraid you'll have to buy another couple of bottles. Still, we haven't done too badly so far.

The best available control for botrytis is thiophanate-methyl, which is contained in Murphy Systemic Fungicide. This can happily be mixed with dimethoate (Murphy Systemic Insecticide) which will control aphids very effectively.

Use the mixture four times during the season, when the first erect buds show, when the first flower opens, at petal fall and again after harvesting.

Aphids: they can be seen clustering under the leaves and at the base of the leaf stalks. The spray programme will control them.

Red spider mite: these minute creatures make small whitish patches on the leaves, followed by bronzing and 'webbing'. The spray programme will control them.

Slugs: almost inevitably, slugs will attack ripening fruits, even if a mulch is used round the plants. They can be quite easily controlled with slug pellets which are no problem to pets or to birds since the crop will be netted.

Botrytis: shows as a grey mould on fruit and stems and is at its worst in cold, wet weather. Remove any fruits that show symptoms, though this shouldn't happen if the spray programme is adhered to.

Verticillium wilt: the whole plant wilts and dies. The only way of controlling this is with a preventive application of benomyl (PBI Benlate). Immerse the plants in it at planting time and give them a thorough soaking in the spring following planting. Affected plants should be dug up and burnt.

Virus: a whole range of viruses attack strawberries and the symptoms are varied. They all cause stunting of the plant and a dramatic reduction in crop. For the small gardener, I suppose the only sensible advice after an attack is to dig up and burn the infected plants and buy a strawberry barrel. The most effective method of prevention is to start with clean stock and to assiduously control aphids.

11 RASPBERRIES

I must say, I've never understood why raspberries have remained the poor relations of strawberries in the soft-fruit world. They command nothing like the prices in the shops and yet for me they are the real flavour of summer. They're easy to grow and can be harvested over a long period and they freeze extremely well. In my view, they should be upgraded to Queen of the soft-fruit kingdom. I'll have to start a petition.

Anyway, if you've got the space, this is certainly one fruit that should be regarded as a necessity in every garden. It has to be admitted that they take up more room than strawberries, but they will tolerate a certain amount of shade, so they will often fill a part of the garden where other fruits would fail.

Varieties
This is another fruit that has been the subject of much research which has resulted in a great improvement in varieties. Once again, buy your plants from a specialist grower and insist on plants that carry a Ministry of Agriculture certificate.

There are several new British varieites that have come from the East Malling programme and from the Scottish Crops Research Institute and more seem to be released each year. All are improvements on the old traditional varieties and, nostalgia or no, if it's high yields and quality you're looking for they're the ones to go for. Naturally I have not had time nor space to try them all, but these are some of those I have tried and which have proved themselves to be first class. They are listed in order of ripening.

Malling Promise: a heavy-yielding early variety with bright red fruits of fine flavour. The canes are vigorous and abundant and indeeed can prove too strong on fertile soil.

Glen Clova: another vigorous variety. I have had canes nine feet tall! Crops are very heavy and the flavour is superb. If you can only grow one variety, this is it, since it crops over a long period and can be used for all purposes.

Malling Jewel: a more compact, mid-season variety that yields good crops of very well-flavoured fruits. Shows some resistance to frost damage and to botrytis.

Malling Admiral: a new variety producing strong growth and numerous canes. Crops are good and the fruit is firm and well flavoured. It has shown resistance to spur blight, botrytis and some virus diseases.

Malling Leo: a late variety that I have picked up until the end of August. It crops very heavily and the fruit is excellent in flavour and firmness, making it suitable for all purposes. It is resistant to raspberry aphids, so should have a better chance of escaping virus infection.

Heritage: the heaviest cropping of the autumn-fruiting varieties. The yields are higher than most autumn fruiters, which tend overall to be lower than the summer types. It's also ready for picking a few days later than most other autumn varieties.

Planting

As with all soft fruit, or any other plant for that matter, you'll reap whatsoever you sow. In other words, the better the initial preparation, the more likelihood there is of healthy plants and high yields.

Prepare the site by digging out a trench at least 2ft (60cm.) wide and one spade deep.

Break up the bottom to the full depth of the fork and put a generous layer of manure, compost or one of the organic alternatives in the bottom. Before refilling the trench, work a bit more organic matter into the soil you have dug out, plus a sprinkling of bonemeal over the top. The soil should now be allowed to settle for a couple of weeks before planting.

Set the plants a little deeper than they grew on the nursery and about 18in. (45cm.) apart, and firm them in well with your boot. The rows should be not less than 6ft (1.8m.) apart. After planting, cut the canes down to leave them 9in. (23cm.) long, to encourage healthy young growth from the base. It's not a good idea to allow canes to fruit in the first year since they then struggle to do both jobs with the result that the new canes are generally weak and spindly. Better curb your impatience and give them a year to settle in.

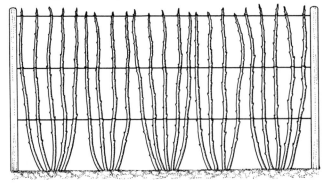

69 *The traditional method of training raspberries is in a single row on wires 6ft (1.8m.) high*

Support and training

The traditional way of training raspberries is to tie them in to wires supported on posts, with the top wire about 6ft (1.8m.) high (69).

Fencing posts are ideal, and they should be 8ft (2.5m.) long sunk 2ft (60cm.) into the ground. It's essential that they should be firm, so either concrete them in, or support them with struts. The posts should be set about 10ft (3m.) apart. Three wires are usually sufficient, with the first about 2ft (60cm.) from the ground, one at the top of the post and one in the middle. The canes are then tied to the wires to form a single row.

The disadvantage with this system is that, since raspberries fruit on one-year-old wood, the new cane is growing up at the same time as the fruiting cane and it tends to become over-crowded. Picking and pruning at the end of the season becomes something of a problem.

With this in mind, I've been trying out a new system of training that has proved highly successful. Instead of growing the canes in one single row, they are splayed out to two low wires at either side of the row allowing the new cane to grow up in the middle unimpeded. There's better air circulation, improved light and picking and pruning are much easier (70).

I use 6ft (1.8m.) posts driven 2ft (60cm.) into the ground 18in. (45cm.) either side of the row. A single wire is stretched along the top of the posts and the canes are tied in to them at about 4in. (10cm.) intervals. The tops are then bent down and tied in horizontally to the wire, all pointing in one direction. During the season, as the canes grow, they are simply tucked in amongst the tied-down canes. The new cane grows straight upwards in the middle of the fruiting canes, leaving all the fruit well presented on the outside of the rows where it is easy to pick.

If your plants are to be grown alongside a fence, you simply use half the system, putting the supporting posts 18in.

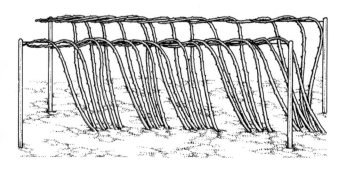

70 *To allow the new cane to grow unimpeded, canes are splayed out to 4ft (1.2m.) high wires and tied down*

(45cm.) out from the fence and tying the canes into a wire running along the top. If the fence faces north or east, the new canes will tend to grow outwards away from the fence, but they are easily held back out of the way of the fruiting canes with a loop of string.

Pruning

Once the fruit has been harvested, the old, fruited cane should be cut out, right down at ground level. The new cane is then tied in its place, so that there is one about every 4in. (10cm.). All weak canes should be removed entirely even if this means that the tied-in canes are more widely spaced.

In the second and subsequent years after planting, the surface roots will spread widely and they'll produce plenty of young shoots wherever they feel like it. They're no respecters of a tidy garden, believe me. Any that encroach into the paths should be removed. The best way to do this is to pull them out bodily. You may well find that in doing so, you remove a lot of root as well, but this won't worry the plants unduly. If you pull them out, the amount of cane produced in the paths tends to diminish year by year, while if you cut them off, like the Hydra, they will only increase.

Autumn-fruiting varieties

Autumn fruiters are treated rather differently both in pruning and training. With these, fruit is produced on canes made during the current year.

They are also much weaker in growth than the summer fruiters.

They are pruned right down to the ground in February and they need little support. In most situations, you'll probably get away with no support at all, but in a windy spot, you may have to run a wire or a length of nylon string either side of the row, just to provide a little moral support. It pays with all plants to make them feel wanted.

Feeding

Raspberries, like strawberries, require little nitrogen, so a general fertiliser is not necessary. I mulch my plants heavily with well-rotted manure or compost every year in February or March, and I supplement this with a dressing of sulphate of potash at about 1oz. per sq. yd (30gm per sq.m.) in February.

If you can't lay your hands on manure and can't make enough compost, then a general fertiliser is in order. But don't overdo it. Blood, fish and bone at 2oz. per sq.yd (60gm per sq.m.) applied in February will serve. The mulching can then be done with grass cuttings during the season as they become available.

Cultivations
The main chore throughout the season is to keep the rows free from weeds. This takes a bit of care, since raspberries are surface-rooting and damage will ensue from deep hoeing. Provided it is directed right down at the base of the plants, there is no reason why annual weeds should not be controlled with the sprayer, using paraquat/diquat (ICI Weedol).

As with most soft fruits, the weight of crop can be dramatically increased by watering during the period when the fruit is beginning to swell. Stop well before it ripens though, or you risk fungus attack.

The fruits are picked when they have coloured up and are pulled off to leave the 'plug' on the plant. They will not store for more than a day or two and it's best to pick over the plants regularly to ensure a fresh supply. They can, of course, be used for jam-making and they will freeze quite well.

Propagation
Really the same rules apply for raspberries as for strawberries only this time I think I would be even more dogmatic. A row of raspberries will last up to ten years, so in my view, it is a false economy to start with canes that may have virus disease.

Much better go to a specialist supplier and buy new canes that are certified free from diseases.

If you do decide to take the risk, the new canes are simply dug up from the pathways with a bit of root.

Pests and diseases
Again, a preventive programme of pest control is called for. Aphids are one of the main problems, not so much because of the damage they cause through sucking the sap, but because of the danger of transmitting virus diseases. Raspberry beetle is another problem in that the small grubs which feed on the ripened fruit are generally not apparent until it's picked when of course, it's too late. They are almost certain to attack, so it's worthwhile guarding against them.

The only nuisance is, and it was bound to happen sooner or later, that the fungicide and insecticide necessary can't be mixed since they come from different manufacturers. It would be possible to concoct another 'cocktail', but this would mean buying yet another bottle. I think it's worthwhile avoiding that and spraying separately.

Aphids: the insects can be seen clustered around the shoot tips and under the leaves. Spray with Murphy Systemic Insecticide or ICI Picket in April and again after flowering. Do not spray within one week of picking.

Raspberry beetle: some shoot damage may be seen, especially on the growing tips, but the main sign of attack is the small maggots in the ripe fruit. Even if no signs are seen, it's worth spraying with Picket when the first flowers open and again at the pink fruit stage.

Spur blight: a common disease, showing as purple blotches on the canes, particularly around the spurs and leaf joints. Spray with Murphy Systemic Fungicide at bud-burst and at fourteen-day intervals until flowering is finished.

Cane spot: shows as small, dark spots on the canes. It is controlled by the spray programme for spur blight.

Botrytis: shows as grey mould on the canes and fruit. Controlled by the spray programme for spur blight.

Virus: again, the main symptom of virus diseases is a general slowing down of growth and marked decrease in crop. It may also show as a mottling on the leaves and the plants generally look sad and yellow. There is no cure, so affected plants must be dug out and burned. Alas, it may also be kept alive in the soil by eelworm, so new plants should not be set in the same spot. Yet another reinforcement for the argument for starting with clean stock and maintaining a regular spray programme against aphids.

12   BRIAR FRUITS

The briar fruits include blackberries, loganberries and a few other crosses known as 'hybrid berries'. They are all grown in exactly the same way, so I've placed them all together in this chapter.

They are all very easy to grow and tolerant of almost any soil or situation, though I must confess that they do take up a fair bit of space and they can be quite uncomfortable because of their thorns. Their great value lies in the fact that they ripen last of all, after the raspberries and they are delicious, eaten fresh or in pies or jam.

Varieties

There are all sorts of weird and wonderful varieties of briar fruits, particularly the hybrid berries and I've fiddled around with quite a few over the years. Many have most seductive sounding names, but produce very little fruit of doubtful value. It has not been difficult to narrow the field down to just three – a blackberry, a loganberry and a hybrid berry. They are certainly the best of each and all you'll need.

Blackberry Ashton Cross: with access to wild blackberries, I have never really seen the point in wasting garden space on them. They are rampant growers and all cultivated varieties lacked the flavour of their wild cousin. That was until Ashton Cross came along. A new variety from East Malling, it produces very high yields of bright, attractive fruits. The berries are not as big as some, but the flavour is as near that of the wild black-berry as you could ever wish for. It's ready for picking from the first week in August until the end of September.

Loganberry L654: oh, I do wish someone would give this poor chap a name! Though it's title may make it sound quite unattractive, it is, in fact, one of the best. A thornless variety, it has been cleaned of virus and so crops extremely well. The fruits are large, red and delicious. It crops from July to mid-August.

Medana Tayberry: undoubtedly the best of the hybrid berries, this new cross between a blackberry and raspberry produces enormous crops. Fruits are large, deep purple and delicious.

Planting

All the briar fruits require a lot of space. They are not too fussy about soil and they will do well in partial shade though they may crop a little later. They must be trained on a framework of wires, supported either on posts or on the fence.

They will survive in poor soil as is evidenced by the wild varieties, but they will do much, much better if the ground is prepared well by deep digging and the incorporation of bulky organic matter.

Plant at least 6ft (1.8m.) apart and preferably 10ft (3m.). Again, cut the stems down to within 9in. (23cm.) of the ground and mulch round the roots with well-rotted manure or compost.

Support and training

All briar fruits are trained against a system of wires supported by posts or fixed to the fence. If you are growing them against the fence or wall, make sure that the wires stand away from the fence by a couple of inches to make tying in easier. With panel fencing, this is just a matter of stapling the wires to the posts, but brick walls will need wooden battens. The wires should start at 3ft (90cm.) from the ground and continue at 1ft (30cm.) intervals to 6ft (1.8m.) high.

There are several alternative methods of training, but the easiest is undoubtedly a fan shape. If you understand the reasons behind the method, it becomes crystal clear.

Like many other soft fruits, the briars fruit on one-year-old wood. So, as with raspberries, it's necessary to grow the fruiting wood and the new wood together. Since, unlike raspberries, the new wood is difficult, at the end of the season, to differentiate from the old, it's advisable to separate them. To do this, the one-year-old wood is splayed out in a fan shape, while the new wood is tied in, as it grows, straight up the centre of the fan (71). At the end of the season, after picking, the old wood is cut out and the new wood trained in a fan shape in its place, and the whole process starts again. It really is not a

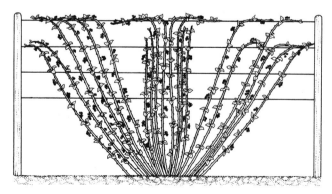

71 *Briar fruits are trained so that the one-year-old fruiting wood is splayed out in a fan, while the new wood is trained in the centre*

difficult system at all, but you do have to keep on top of that young wood. It grows quite fast in the summer and will need to be kept under control by tying it in about once a fortnight.

Cultivations

Use exactly the same feeding programme as recommended for raspberries. There should certainly be enough nitrogen in the mulch to provide more than adequate growth of stems and leaves, but again, potash will generally need to be added.

I think that, if anything, mulching is more important with briars than with raspberries. A good thick mulch, apart from adding nutrients, is very effective in keeping down weeds. If you are growing any of the spiny varieties, you will not want to do too much hand weeding, believe me.

The same watering rules apply. If you have a dryish spell when the fruits are beginning to swell, it pays hands down to water artificially.

Propagation

If I seem to be continually trying to put you off home-propagation, forgive me, but bear in mind that the briars suffer from virus diseases too. If you are determined to raise your own replacements, ensure that you start with clean stock and keep up the war against aphids.

If you allow a shoot from any of the briars to trail on the ground, like as not it will form roots, so propagation is not a difficult matter. Simply take out a small hole and bury one of the young tips of a shoot. Cover it with soil and it will root readily. It can be severed from mother in the spring and replanted (72).

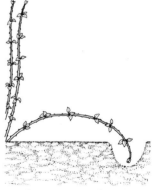

72 *Propagate new plants by burying a tip about 6in. (15cm.) deep. When it starts to shoot it can be severed from the parent*

Pests and diseases

Briars suffer the same pests and diseases as raspberries and the treatment is the same. If anything, they are less prone, but it's worthwhile keeping up the spray programme just in case.

Birds: I'm sure that birds like briar fruits more than any other. They seem to be especially fond of tayberries and I found, in the first season of growing them, that I picked not a single berry. They'll get there long before you do, so it's essential to net them.

13 BLACKCURRANTS

Long recommended for their health-giving properties, black-currants are a must for the family garden. Packed with Vitamin C, they'll guarantee that little Johnny is even more objectionably active than ever. One of the most versatile of fruits, they can be eaten fresh, stewed, bottled, jammed or frozen. They make terrific wine and the juice, mixed with dry white wine is a favourite aperitif in France. They are easy to grow and produce heavy crops just about every year. On the debit side, they take up a fair bit of room and they are, I'm afraid, subject to virus diseases.

Varieties

The popularity of blackcurrant juice has made them a profitable crop for fruit farmers, so there has been plenty of research into new varieties. Though the earlier new introductions lacked, for me, some of the flavour of the traditional favourites, the latest batch of new recruits lacks nothing. In my view they far outclass their ancestors.

You may have to search for some of them but they are all available from specialist growers. Again, they are subject to the Ministry Certification scheme.

Ben More: the latest flowering variety available and therefore stands a better chance of avoiding frost damage. Crops are very heavy and quality and flavour excellent. Certainly the one to go for if you only want one variety.

Ben Lomond: much like Ben More except that it flowers a little earlier. It has produced heavier crops in the south of England which could make it a better bet for that area.

Malling Jet: another late-flowering variety, it has the distinction of producing its fruit on very long sprigs so picking is easier and less arduous. Its fruits have perhaps the longest staying power of all varieties, hanging on the bush for a long time before deteriorating. A valuable asset for the busy gardener who may not be able to pick the fruit just when it's at its best. The flavour is not as strong as many other varieties.

Planting

Though they will tolerate partial shade, blackcurrants will do much better in a sunny spot. Here is one plant that will really repay heavy manuring and good soil preparation, so deep digging, working in manure or compost is the order of the day.

If you suspect your soil of being either very acid or very alkaline, it will pay you to take a soil test. Blackcurrants will not grow successfully in either condition so aim for a pH of 6.5. Plant the bushes 5ft (1.5m.) apart and, if you decide on more than one row, allow at least 6ft (1.8m.) between the rows. They are generally grown as 'stooled' plants which means that, instead of growing them on a central stem as you would redcurrants or gooseberries, you try to encourage strong young growths right from the base of the plant. So, when planting, aim to set the plants so that they are about 1in. (2.5cm.) lower in the ground than they grew on the nursery.

The best fruit is produced on one-year-old wood, so the aim should be to get as much as possible to grow in the first year to give a bumper crop the year after. After planting, to encourage this strong growth, cut all the stems right down to within one bud from the ground. This may seem a bit drastic at the time, but it will result in much stronger young growth (73).

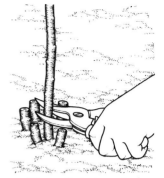

73 *Plant a little deeper than they grew on the nursery and afterwards, prune right down to the ground*

Feeding

Unlike the soft fruits mentioned so far, blackcurrants will respond well to higher levels of nitrogen, so a general fertiliser can be used to advantage. Blood, fish and bone should be applied in February at about 4oz. per sq. yd (120gm per sq. m.). If growth seems poor during the year, give them another feed at the same rate during May.

An annual mulch with manure or compost should provide the trace elements required.

Pruning

In the first winter after planting, there is little to do. Simply go round the bushes and remove any shoots that are weak, damaged or overcrowded. After fruiting, which will be in the second summer after planting and every year subsequently, pruning should be severe. Cut back all the one-year-old shoots that have borne fruit, to within one bud of the base. This seemingly draconian measure will encourage strong growth from the base, which is where you want it to give the longest fruit-bearing stems possible (74).

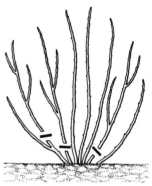

74 *After fruiting, the old wood that has borne fruit should be cut right out*

If there is not a lot of new wood growing right from the bottom of the plant, you may find it necessary to prune back to a strong, low side-shoot on the old wood.

I always make my picking operation easier by combining it with the pruning. Once the fruit is ripe and ready for picking, I prune the old stems out and pick the fruit off them later, sitting down in the sun. It does the plants no harm, and my back a power of good.

Cultivations

Apart from the annual mulch already mentioned, the only chore during the season is to keep the plants weed-free. They are very shallow rooting and need all the roots they can get to make that strong young growth each year. So if you use the hoe, make sure it only tills the top half an inch or so. I prefer to use weedkiller for annual weeds, but of course, great care must be exercised here to avoid it drifting onto the plants.

Again, watering will increase the weight of the crop if applied as the fruits are swelling. Once they get near the colouring stage, avoid wetting the fruits for fear of fungus attack.

Propagation

At the risk of boring you, I'll repeat my oft-heard virus warning. Blackcurrants are subject to them too.

Propagation is done by hardwood cuttings taken in the autumn. Take young shoots of the current season's growth and about 8in. (20cm.) long (75). Trim them below a bud at the base and just above one at the top to remove the soft tip. Cut a small slit trench in an out-of-the-way corner of the garden and line the bottom with a little silver sand (76). Push the cuttings in to leave only two or three buds showing and close the trench, firming the cuttings in with your boot (77). Note that no buds have been removed, since these will grow out under the soil to make the 'stool'. Most of the cuttings will have rooted by the following autumn when they can be transplanted to their permanent positions.

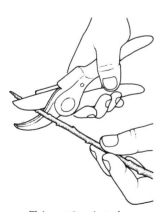

75 *Trim cuttings just above a bud at the top and just below at the bottom, making the cutting about 8in. (20cm.) long*

76 *Cut a narrow slit trench and line it with silver or sharp sand*

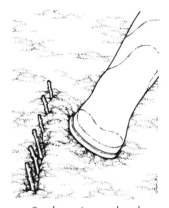

77 *Set the cuttings so that they rest on the sand leaving two or three buds above soil level. Firm them in well*

Pests and diseases

Again it is necessary to control aphids to guard against virus infection, but unfortunately, the story is more complicated with blackcurrants. They are infected with virus by another pest called big-bud mite, for which there is no control. Constant vigilance is called for together with perhaps a ritual sacrifice of a packet of frozen blackcurrants at harvest time. A spray programme is advisable for aphids, but since mildew, the most serious of the fungus diseases attacking blackcurrants, is not inevitable, it is only necessary to mix a 'cocktail' if it's visible.

Aphids: the insects can be seen clustered under the leaves and on shoot tips and some types cause an unsightly red or yellow blistering of the leaves. Spray with ICI Picket at fortnightly intervals except during flowering.

Big-bud mite: this little blighter is the bane of a blackcurrant grower's life. It attacks the buds causing them to swell to about twice their normal size, and it is the carrier of the virus. The only control is to check over the bushes in January or February and remove any enlarged buds.

If the attack is really severe, it may become necessary to dig up the bushes and burn them.

Sawfly: a pest that is more troublesome on gooseberries, but may attack blackcurrants too. They are small green things with black spots and they're very, very hungry indeed. They can comfortably strip a bush of its foliage in a day. Keep a careful eye on the bushes, bearing in mind that they generally start towards the centre of the bush. If you see one, spray immediately with Picket. Even then, they may attack again, so don't be lulled into a false sense of security. Of course, if you're spraying regularly against greenfly, there should be little trouble from sawfly.

Leaf spot: this fungus disease first shows as small brown spots on the leaves. These eventually merge together and the whole leaf turns brown and falls early. It is controlled by spraying with ICI Nimrod 'T' after flowering and then at two-week intervals.

Mildew: causes a white, powdery deposit on leaves and shoot-tips generally towards the end of the season. Spray it when seen with Nimrod 'T'.

Birds: almost inevitably, birds will strip not only the fruits but the young buds as well. I have tried most recognised controls and find that the only guaranteed method is to net the bushes.

14 GOOSEBERRIES

As the earliest soft fruit of the year, the humble goosegog is as welcome as the buds in May. They are very soil-tolerant and easy to grow and they can be trained as cordons along a fence where they occupy very little space.

Redcurrants and white currants are grown in exactly the same way, so I have included them here.

Varieties

I suppose that it's true to say that neither gooseberries nor red-currants are as widely grown commercially as other fruits so there has not been so much research into new varieties. A couple of new gooseberries have appeared in the last few years and they are a great improvement on the older favourites.

White currants are very much a minority crop though I think that their distinctive flavour makes them well worth growing if space is available. I wouldn't mind betting that the single variety that appears to be all that's available has been around for donkey's years.

Whitesmith: a fairly early gooseberry giving high yields of large, oval berries which are pale green with a yellow tinge. One of the best all-round varieties.

Jubilee: a new variety from East Malling, this mid-season gooseberry is very similar to the most popular variety *Careless* and should, I think, replace it. It has been cleaned of virus infections so will produce heavier crops of large, yellow fruits which can be used for all culinary purposes as well as fresh from the bush when fully ripe. It is also resistant (though not immune) to mildew.

Invicta: another new variety that may prove a bit hard to find. It's worth searching out. It produces very high yields, is resistant to mildew and free from virus. The berries are large and white with an excellent flavour and good for all purposes. If it has a snag, it is that the vigorous, rather spreading bushes are covered in large, pretty vicious spines.

Redcurrant Red Lake: certainly the best-flavoured and heaviest cropping variety available. It crops mid-season and the fruit is sweet and juicy and borne on long, easy-to-pick sprigs.

White Currant White Versailles: as far as I know, the only variety available. A fairly heavy cropper and early, producing long sprigs of yellowish white berries with a distinctive flavour.

There is no certification scheme for gooseberries or red and white currants but this is not a problem since virus rarely attacks. Nonetheless, it is still better to buy good, healthy stock from a specialist grower.

Planting

Gooseberries and currants will tolerate some shade, but they will do best in a sunny spot. It is important to prepare the land well by deep digging with the incorporation of bulky organic matter, providing good drainage and an ability to retain water and nutrients.

Removal of perennial weeds such as couch grass and bind-weed is vital, especially with gooseberries, since the spines make hand weeding a hazardous operation. If even small quantities of either of these pernicious weeds are present, they should be sprayed out with Tumbleweed before preparing the ground for planting.

Plant 5ft (1.5m.) apart with 6ft (1.8m.) between the rows.

Unlike blackcurrants, they are grown on a leg to facilitate weeding underneath and to prevent the more drooping varieties from touching the ground. Before planting, check to see if there are any suckers arising from the roots and pull them off. Plant just a little lower than they grew on the nursery.

After planting, mulch with a generous dressing of manure or compost round the plants but not actually touching the stems. To encourage strong stem growth the following year, the branches should be cut back after planting to a strong bud to leave about half the current year's growth. Red and white currants and upright varieties of gooseberry should be pruned back to an outward or downward-facing bud, but drooping varieties of gooseberry should be pruned to an upward-facing one.

Feeding

While high levels of nitrogen are not necessary, gooseberries and currants are very prone to potash deficiency. Each February they should be given a feed at about 1oz. per sq. yd (30gm per sq.m.). If they show signs of browning on the margins of the leaves, this is probably due to a potash deficiency and they should then be given an extra dressing at the same rate straight away.

An annual mulch of well-rotted manure or compost should provide the other necessary nutrients, though if the plants look as though they are not growing well, they can be given a general fertiliser in the spring instead of the potash feed, applied at about 4oz. per sq.yd (120gm per sq.m.).

Pruning

The aim of early pruning is to make a strong growing, cup-shaped bush that is more or less open in the middle. For the first three years after planting, cut back the growing point of each branch to leave about half of the previous season's growth. Side-shoots are cut back to about 3in. (7.5cm.). Any branches that are broken, overcrowded or growing into the centre of the bush are removed altogether.

After three years, you will have built up a good, strong, well-shaped bush and pruning can then take place in the summer. At about the end of June, all the side-shoots are reduced to five leaves or so. If the growing point of each branch has reached the required length, it can be treated like a side-shoot and cut back to five leaves too.

Cultivations

There's little to do really, during the season, except weeding and, when the fruit begins to swell, watering. It's important, especially with currants, to protect the bushes from birds. Remember that they are very fond of the fruit buds of both currants and gooseberries, so this means netting all bushes from early on in the year. The best bet is to grow them in the safety of a fruit cage.

Cordons

If space is at a premium, gooseberries, red and white currants make excellent cordons. They are grown slightly differently from apple or pear cordons, but the basic principles are the same.

It is possible to buy ready-started cordons from a fruit specialist, or you can buy maiden bushes and start your own. They are grown as single, double or triple cordons, in other words with one, two or three main stems. It doesn't make a lot of difference which you choose, and I favour doubles as a good old English compromise.

They need to be grown up a structure of wires, either fixed to the fence or to posts. Three wires are sufficient about 1ft (30cm.) and 6ft (1.8m.) from the ground with one in the middle.

If you are starting from scratch, decide first of all how many branches you intend to grow from each plant and plant them so that there will be 1ft (30cm.) between each branch. In other words, single cordons will be planted 1ft (30cm.) apart, doubles 2ft (60cm.) and triples 3ft (90cm.) (78). After planting, wire bamboo canes to the wires in the positions of the branches that will eventually be trained in.

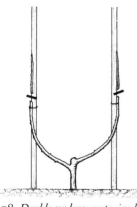

78 *Double cordons are trained to carry two 'arms' at about 1ft (30cm.) apart. In winter, prune the leaders back by about a third*

If your maiden plant has two strong, well-placed side-shoots, they can be used as the side-branches. Cut them back immediately after planting to about two or three buds. For double cordons remove the centre growth to just above the two branches or, if you decide to grow triples, cut this leading shoot back to three buds (79). Single cordons are cut back by about half and any side-shoots to about 1in. (2.5cm.).

In the summer, the side-shoots are allowed to grow out until they reach the canes and are then tied in to them with their tips pointing upwards.

In the second winter, these main stems are cut back by about a third to promote strong growth the next year.

In the next and subsequent summers, pruning is aimed at making short fruiting spurs on the side branches. About the end of June, they are all reduced to five leaves, but the leader is left alone until it reaches the top of the cane.

In the following and subsequent winters, those side-shoots are further reduced to leave just two buds, while the leader is cut back by about a third. When the leader reaches the top, treat it like a side-shoot.

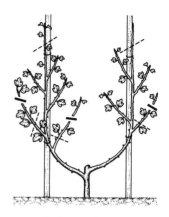

79 *Side-shoots will grow on each branch and these are cut back to five leaves in June. In the winter, prune them further to leave two buds and prune the leader by a third*

Propagation

Redcurrants and white currants grow more vigorously than gooseberries and they will root from cuttings with the greatest of ease, so there is no need for the rather more pernickety methods used for gooseberries.

Hardwood cuttings are taken in October or November, selecting strong young wood of the current season's growth. The cuttings should be at least 10in. (25cm.) and preferably 12in. (30cm.) long and should be cleanly cut back to just below a bud at the bottom and just above one at the top.

Since the plants are to be grown on a short stem, we want to avoid suckers coming from below the ground, so all but the top five buds are removed.

The cuttings are then put into slit trenches in the same way as described for blackcurrants (page 86) and should be ready for transplanting the following autumn.

Gooseberries don't root so readily so the technique is somewhat different. It has been found that the best time to take the cuttings is in September, before the leaves have fallen. Take them in the same way as redcurrants, but don't remove the buds from the bottom. They will root much better if they are left on, but of course, this presents the problem of suckers. When the plants are rooted and subsequently lifted the following autumn, before replanting, any suckers that arise from the roots should be pulled off. You may find that more arise after planting, and these will have to be removed as close to the roots as possible. They can generally be pulled away quite easily. At Barnsdale, out of twenty cuttings taken in this way, seventeen rooted to make excellent young plants.

Pests and diseases

Fortunately, redcurrants, white currants and gooseberries are not too prone to bad attacks from many of the pests and diseases of blackcurrants. However, there are two particularly bad ones and they must be controlled immediately they are seen. There is no need for a regular spray programme.

Aphids: the insects can be seen clustered round the shoot tips and under the leaves. Spray with ICI Picket or Murphy Systemic Insecticide as soon as they are seen.

Sawfly: these small green, spotted caterpillars don't attack every year, but when they do they make a job of it. Keep a watchful eye for damaged leaves and spray with Picket immediately.

Mildew: the American Gooseberry Mildew is certainly the most common and the most devastating of gooseberry troubles. It forms a white, or greyish furry deposit on leaves, stems and fruits. If left unchecked, it will completely cover the bushes, slowing growth and ruining fruit. As soon as you see the first signs, spray with ICI Nimrod 'T', and repeat the dose a fortnight later.

Leaf spot: the same disease that attacks blackcurrants but not generally so common. If the dark spots are seen, spray with Nimrod 'T'.

Birds: as I have already pointed out, gooseberries and currants are all subject to attack from birds – particularly bullfinches – during the late winter when they strip the buds, and also at fruiting time. Netting is the only answer and a fruit cage is ideal.

15 GRAPES

It has to be said that grapes are not the most reliable of fruits to grow outside. In a bad year when the late summer is wet and sunless, they may fail to ripen and are likely to be attacked by mildew. Late frosts can kill flowers and will even damage young shoots.

Having said that, we should remind ourselves that Britain was a major wine-producing country before the dissolution of the monasteries by Henry VIII, and things were even more difficult then for vine growers than they are now. New varieties and more sophisticated methods have brought grape growing back to fashion, particularly in the southern half of the country. The furthest north I know of a vineyard is Yorkshire, and I'm quite prepared to believe that successful growers exist even further north. Certainly, if you live south of the Humber and wish to grow grapes for wine, there is no reason at all why you shouldn't. But be prepared for the odd failure every so often.

Varieties
You will have to dig out a vine specialist for the best varieties, but there are several professional grape growers who will also supply plants. With a few exceptions, green grapes are more likely to succeed, especially in the north.

While grapes are technically self-fertile, they'll set better if pollinated by another variety that flowers at the same time.

Madeleine Angevine: a strong grower and a heavy cropper, this variety is one of the more suitable ones for northerly areas. The grapes are small and sweet and make a high-quality wine.

Muller Thurgau: probably the most widely-planted outdoors. It really needs a fair amount of sun but in a good year gives very heavy crops of fine quality grapes.

Siegerrebe: a very early-ripening variety giving good crops of high quality fruit. However, it is fairly subject to botrytis attack. It can be used for eating or wine-making.

Seyve-Villard: a vigorous variety producing heavy crops of golden grapes of very high quality. It really needs a limy soil and a good year.

Brant: a red variety, very strong growing and rarely failing to produce a heavy crop of small, sweet grapes. The fruit is good for both eating fresh and for wine-making. They have the added ornamental advantage of fine autumn colour.

There are, of course, other varieties which are widely grown by commercial growers but rarely offered to gardeners. If you are lucky enough to live near a vineyard, it would be well worthwhile taking further advice and, if possible, buying a few plants of varieties known to do well locally. You may well feel obliged to buy a case of wine in return for advice, but I can think of worse penalties!

Planting
Vines, more than any other soft fruit, need sun. Ideally they should be grown against a warm, south-facing wall, where they will receive the double benefit of protection from the wind and the 'storage-heater' effect of the brick.

They don't need a rich soil, but good drainage is essential. On heavy, waterlogged soils they will not do well. So, dig out a good trench and break up the bottom. If the soil is heavy, it will pay to put some drainage material like old brick rubble in the bottom of the trench.

With extra-good drainage, they will need a bit of help to get sufficient water for their needs, so some form of organic matter is advisable. Though it is often recommended that manure or compost is too rich in nitrogen, I have found no adverse results. The theory is that too much nitrogen encourages rank growth at the expense of fruit. Frankly, by the time the vine is in a position to produce grapes, the nitrogen in the manure is long gone.

Grapes do best on a limey soil, so it pays to take a soil test. If the pH is lower than 6.5, add lime in the spring.

Planting should be done in the autumn and certainly not later than January. Plant 5ft (1.5m.) apart with 6ft (1.8m.) between rows. If you are planting against a wall, bear in mind that the soil often dries out badly right near the wall, so plant a foot or so out from it. In the early stages after planting, you may well have to water by hand until the plant puts out roots far enough from the wall to get adequate moisture.

Most vines are budded onto a rootstock, so plant at a depth that ensures that the joint between stock and variety is well above soil level. After planting, mulch with manure or compost.

Support and training
Vines will need the support of wires, which are either fixed to the wall or fence or supported on posts. The bottom wire should be about 18in. (45cm.) above the ground, the top wire 4ft (1.2m.) high with one in the middle. Put a stout post at each planting position.

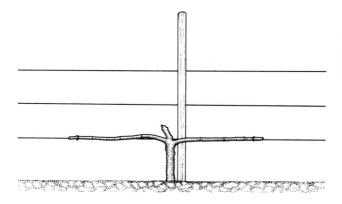

80 *In the first winter after planting, two shoots are tied in to the wires either side of the centre cane, and the centre shoot is cut back to three buds*

81 *The following summer, tie the new growth to the centre post. The side-shoots produced from the two arms are tied in and any shoots from these, pinched back to one leaf*

Immediately after planting and well before the end of January at the latest, prune the cane back to leave three strong buds. The reason for pruning when the plant is dormant is that, once it starts growing, it will bleed from the pruning cut and this will severely weaken the plant.

During the first summer, allow the three shoots to grow, tying them loosely to the centre stake. Pinch back side-shoots to one or two buds as they develop and, in September, pinch out the soft growing tips.

In the following winter, select the two strongest shoots and tie these in to the bottom wire, one either side of the stake. They should be pruned back to about 2½ft (75cm.). The remaining shoot is pruned back hard to leave three buds (80).

The following summer, the centre three shoots are tied in loosely to the stake as last summer. The two tied-in side-branches will produce upward growing shoots and it is on these that the fruit is produced (81).

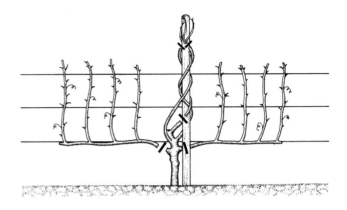

82 *The following winter, cut out the arms that have borne fruit, tie in the two replacement arms and prune the centre shoot back to three buds*

Tie them in to the three wires and pinch back side-shoots as before, leaving one leaf. When they reach the top of the wire, trim the tops off.

Fruit will be produced on these shoots but you will have to brace yourself to allow only about four bunches per vine in the first fruiting year or they will be permanently weakened. Later, take one bunch per shoot.

At the end of the season, the whole process starts again. The fruited branches are cut right out, the three replacements growing up the stake are tied into their place with the weakest one being pruned back to three buds again (82).

Feeding

Despite the threats of too much growth, I always mulch in the early spring with well-rotted manure or compost. This should be sufficient feed unless the plants look unhappy and are not growing well. Then a feed with a general fertiliser in February will be necessary. I must say that I have never had to do it and, contrary to popular opinion, the Barnsdale soil is not the most fertile in the world, so I would doubt that regular feeding would normally be necessary. On poor soil use blood, fish and bone at about 3oz. per sq.yd (90gm per sq.m.).

Cultivations

Shallow hoeing will be necessary to keep down weeds, and water should be applied in dry weather, especially if the vines are growing against a wall. If you are watering with a sprinkler, stop when the grapes begin to swell or you risk fungus attack.

Grapes being grown for eating fresh will need to be thinned or they will be too small for comfort. Start soon after the bunches have set and use a pair of small scissors. Special vine scissors are ideal, though a pair of nail scissors will do. Remove any badly-shaped berries first and then, when they are about the size of a pea, cut out enough to allow the remainder to swell to a reasonable size. This will vary a bit from variety to variety, but you'll get the hang of it easily in the second year when you know what to expect. Outdoor grapes will never be as large as indoor ones, so don't expect miracles. If you are growing purely for wine, thinning is unnecessary, though it will still pay to nip any off that are attacked by fungus.

Protection

Grapes do well grown in a polythene greenhouse or under large cloches. The one snag is that fungus diseases will be a lot more at home in the poorly ventilated conditions. If they are grown under glass barn cloches, the centre replacement stems can grow up through a space in the middle between the panes, but under polythene cloches, it's not that easy. You'll have to devise a different method by which the replacement shoots are trained in to a higher horizontal wire.

Pests and diseases

Though vines are not subject to attack from many pests, fungus diseases have a field day, and this is the main concern. There are two main culprits and these can be controlled with a spray programme using Murphy Systemic Fungicide at fortnightly intervals from mid-June, but suspending spraying during the flowering period.

Wasps: attack the fruits with undiluted venom. There's not a lot you can do short of trapping them. I have found the most effective method to be the good old-fashioned jam-jar of stale beer. Sink it into the ground and you'll no doubt bag a few slugs as well.

Birds: I sometimes think we need a Royal Society for the Protection of Gardeners rather than worrying about birds. Again, they can be a big problem and the only effective answer is to net the vines against them.

Mildew: causes whitish patches on leaves and stems. It is at its worst when the plants are suffering from dryness at the roots. Control by following the spray programme.

Botrytis: the grey mould fungus so common on many other plants will attack shoots, buds and particularly fruit, covering it with a grey felt. Control by removing infected fruit as soon as it's seen and by following the spray programme.

INDEX